South Africa: WORKERS UNDER APARTHEID

Alex. Hepple

Published for the International Defence and Aid Fund
by Christian Action Publications Ltd
2 Amen Court, London, E.C.4

London 1969

CONTENTS

INTRODUCTION

On March 11, 1964 the South African Government announced its withdrawal from the International Labour Organisation Three months later the ILO unanimously adopted a Declaration on apartheid in South Africa and a Programme for its elimination. These documents specified the ways in which laws and practices in South Africa violated the principles of the ILO and the changes that should be made to ensure equality of opportunity, freedom of association, and freedom of choice of employment and occupation.

South Africa's resignation from the ILO became effective on March 11, 1966, from which date complaints against it have been referred to the United Nations. There are now innumerable statements, declarations and resolutions on the subject of apartheid, all of which are treated with contempt by the South African Government. The UN Special Committee on the Policies of Apartheid attributes the failure of the UN to remedy the situation largely to the main trading partners of South Africa, who continue to bolster up the present regime by continuing their lucrative trade with the Republic. The Committee says the reluctance of these states to join in effective international action, and the collaboration of powerful foreign economic and financial interests with the South African Government, have encouraged it to persist in its apartheid policies.

Even the arms embargo imposed by the UN Security Council in 1964 has done little more than irritate the South African Government; and the British Conservative Party has comforted South Africa with the promise to resume the supply of armaments when elected to power.

With the aid of foreign investors, South Africa is steadily expanding her industrial output and export of manufactured goods. The increased production is being achieved by the labour of non-white workers; and costs are held down by a low-wage structure, based on a directed African labour force, disciplined by harsh, unjust, discriminatory laws and practices. This is the essence of apartheid.

Far from heeding the ILO and UN calls to respect the freedom and dignity of all human beings, irrespective of race, the South African Government is continually intensifying the exploitation of African workers. New measures have stripped a vast number of Africans of the right to permanent employment and a settled life in the urban areas, reducing them to the status of migrants; the unemployed may be ordered out of the only areas where work is available; the aged, the disabled and the infirm are removed to rural settlements, far from the places where they have laboured for the best part of their lives in the service of the white man.

This book explains how apartheid fosters economic exploitation of South Africa's non-white workers and keeps them poor; how it limits their job opportunities, retards their advancement, and represses their right to organise and bargain with their employers. It also tells how the government is making rightless migrants of urban Africans, to maintain a system of disciplined, directed and cheap labour.

Part One outlines the political background of the present Government's policy. Part Two describes the labour force, its racial grading and the various laws designed to control and discipline African workers. Part Three deals with the labour laws applying to collective bargaining, wage fixing, the right to strike and the reservation of jobs on a racial basis. Part Four tells the story of trade unionism and the ways in which the unionisation of Africans is curbed by repressive action by the authorities. The final Part records the steps taken by the International Labour Organisation and the United Nations to deal with the labour and trade union situation in South Africa.

Part One

The Background

1. Two Labour Codes

South Africa has two labour codes. These express the country's policy of racial discrimination in employment and labour organisation.

The more favourable code, which applies to less than half the economically active population—the white, Coloured and Indian workers—embodies strict requirements for the application of apartheid in trade unions and imposes severe restraints upon access to employment, the freedom to organise, to strike, and to take political action.

The second code, which applies to the majority of South Africa's working class—the Africans—pegs them to servitude. A mass of " Bantu " laws and regulations are woven into the fabric of the code for African workers, directing their labour according to the desires of white authority. These laws frustrate Africans in their efforts to earn a living and keep them in a perpetual state of insecurity.

In addition to the " Bantu " laws, Africans are subject to various labour laws which impose additional handicaps upon them. They are not permitted to engage in collective bargaining through the industrial council system, like other workers. The government is firmly opposed to the unionisation of African workers and refuses to give legal status to their trade unions. Strikes are prohibited under heavy penalties. Disputes with their employers cannot be argued and resolved by African workers themselves but must be settled by government officials.

The two codes were not conceived as a specific plan. They developed gradually from the time the white man first began to seek ways and means of harnessing the vast potential non-white labour force in Southern Africa. With the discovery of diamonds and gold, special measures were taken for the recruitment and disciplining of African miners, including regulations for their housing in fenced-in compounds.

In the period of rapid industrialisation during and after the Second World War, the white government felt compelled to extend the scope and severity of laws affecting the movement and employment of Africans

In spite of restrictions on entry, lack of housing and other obstacles, the influx of Africans into the urban areas was considerable. On the Witwatersrand, the African population almost doubled between 1936 and 1948, rising from 600,000 to about 1,000,000. Without this migration there could have been little economic progress. Industry, commerce and the services were in desperate need of labour.

It was at this juncture, in 1948, that the Afrikaner Nationalist Party came to power. Under the premiership first of Dr. D. F. Malan, then Mr. J. G. Strydom and soon afterwards Dr. H. F. Verwoerd, the Nationalist rulers sharpened the teeth of old racial laws and made new enactments to entrench the mastery of the whites and the servitude of the blacks.

2. Broederbond—Nationalist Aims

Long before coming to power, the Nationalist Party had its apartheid labour policy prepared. Its chief architects were the energetic members of the Afrikaner Broederbond, a secret society with the objective of a " Christian-National republican state " under the domination of Afrikaners. The Broederbond concept was a strictly disciplined nation in which segregation of the races was to be fully enforced. More than half its members belonged to the Nationalist Party. Its executive committee, referred to as " The Twelve Apostles ", included Dr. H. F. Verwoerd, Dr. T. E. Donges, Dr. Albert Hertzog and Dr. N. Diederichs and others who later became Cabinet Ministers.

Two South African Prime Ministers felt obliged to warn the nation of the machinations of the Broederbond-Nationalist alliance. In November 1935, General J. B. M. Hertzog (father of Dr. Albert Hertzog) declared " the secret Broederbond is nothing else but a purified Nationalist Party busy underground, and the Purified Nationalist Party is nothing else but a secret Afrikaner Broederbond continuing its activities above ground ".

Nine years later General Smuts described the Broederbond as " a dangerous, cunning, political, fascist organisation . . . whose control, policy, membership and activities are strictly secret, and form a sort of Gestapo ".

The Broederbond pursued a carefully prepared plan to gain control of Afrikaner organisations, through which to propagate its aims. It succeeded in linking all Afrikaans cultural organisations in the Federasie van Afrikaanse Kultuurverenigings* (FAK) and made this body the instrument through which to establish other organisations, each with a specific task of indoctrinating Afrikaners towards the achievement of the Broederbond aims. From 1938 onwards, a number of FAK subsidiaries came into existence. One of these was the Blankewerkersbeskermingsbond† (BWBB). Its membership was restricted to white Protestants; its objects, " founded on the Christian-National traditions of the people of South Africa ", were to combat the " evils " affecting white workers on the Witwatersrand. Its constitution stated that the BWBB aims were the reservation of occupations on a racial basis; no undesirable contact between white and non-white workers in their employment; and the prohibition of racially mixed trade unions.

The head of the BWBB was Senator Jan de Klerk, secretary of the Nationalist Party. In 1953 he was made a Senator, to take over the Party leadership in the Senate from Dr. Verwoerd, who had become a member of the House of Assembly. The following year he was made Minister of Labour. In 1968 he was still in the Cabinet, as Minister of National Education and of Information.

---

*Federation of Cultural Associations.

†White Workers' Protection Society.

The main target of the BWBB was the Garment Workers' Union. In their church and cultural associations the Afrikaner members of the union were incited against the leadership and indoctrinated with racial theories. The BWBB also paid attention to the Mineworkers' Union, the Amalgamated Union of Building Trade Workers (AUBTW) and the Leatherworkers' Union.

Its activities in these unions were greatly helped by Dr. Albert Hertzog, whose diligence secured him honorary membership of the Mineworkers' Union General Council. This success among the white miners resulted mainly from the fact that most of them were Afrikaners who supported the Nationalist Party. Neither the BWBB nor Dr. Hertzog were able to alienate a sufficient number of members of other unions to bring them into the Nationalist camp.

The outbreak of the Second World War in 1939 had temporarily divided Afrikanerdom. The Nationalists under Dr. Malan were opposed to South Africa entering the war. They wanted South Africa to remain neutral, as did General Hertzog, then Prime Minister. The war issue resulted in a realignment of political forces, with the Broederbond-dominated Nationalist Party at the spearhead. In June 1941, an " Afrikaner Front " was announced, in a " Declaration on behalf of the People's Organisations ", proclaiming the common objective of " a free, independent, republican, Christian-National state, based on the word of God, eschewing all foreign models . . . with the strongest emphasis upon the effective disciplining of the people ".

The Declaration was signed by the heads of the various Broederbond subsidiaries, three ministers of the Dutch Reformed churches and the Commandant-General of the Ossewabrandwag (OB) and given the full backing of the Nationalist Party. The Ossewabrandwag (Ox Wagon Sentinel) was a militant, National-Socialist movement which sought the establishment of an authoritarian state, with citizenship restricted to " assimilable white elements ", the abolition of private enterprise and the breaking of the British connection. One of its leaders was the present Prime Minister, Mr. J. B. Vorster, who was interned during the war for his OB activities. In one of his war-time speeches as OB commandant, Mr. Vorster said of the movement's aims :—

> *" We stand for Christian Nationalism, which is an ally of National Socialism. You can call the anti-democratic principle dictatorship if you wish. In Italy it is called Fascism, in Germany National Socialism, and in South Africa Christian Nationalism ".*

In parliament, the Nationalist Party took every opportunity to expound the policy it intended to pursue if elected to rule the country. The first declaration of intent in regard to labour policy came from Mr. B. J. Schoeman, who later became the Minister of Labour in the Nationalist Cabinet of 1948. On March 19, 1942, he stated (1) that wage fixing should be entirely in the hands of the state; (2) that self-government in industry and collective bargaining must be abolished; (3) that racial quotas should be fixed for all skilled, semi-skilled and unskilled occupations.[1]

The following year Mr. Schoeman elaborated on the plan, adding that when it was put into operation :—

> *" . . . the principal function of the trade unions will disappear . . . These organisations will not so much be entrusted with the function of obtaining*

better wages and better working conditions; . . . they will be mainly entrusted with the task of regulating domestic matters, as between the employers and employees. And for the rest, of looking after the spiritual welfare of the workers ".[2]

In their manifesto for the wartime general election of 1943, the Nationalist Party, said of trade unions:—

" Trade unionism on National lines has love and respect for its own culture, language and Church, which it consciously endeavours to cultivate among all the workers within the boundary of the State and perpetuate from generation to generation. Just so shall the Church, the body par excellence, which in the past, concerned itself with the poverty and sufferings of the Afrikaner throw in its weight behind National trade unionism and help to alleviate the lot of the worker ".[3]

The Nationalists were heavily defeated in this election but the Afrikaner people were beginning to respond to the powerful pressures of the Broederbond octopus. In the schools, in cultural societies, in social and sporting activities, and in church circles they were being indoctrinated with persuasive calls to Afrikaner nationalism.

From the political platform, Mr. Schoeman declaimed:—

" . . . There must be changes in the foreign British system, which does not conform to the character and traditions of the Afrikaner . . . the present (labour) system must be destroyed and a new one created . . . "[4]

The Nationalist Party manifesto for the 1948 elections included a labour policy with strong authoritarian overtones. It spoke of the state guarding against workers' organisations " being misused for purposes inimical to the country and its people or in order to disturb the proper and necessary equilibrium between the respective sectional interests in our economic structure ". It promised " a system of State responsibility " to supplement collective bargaining, to be exercised by a Central Economic Council and a Labour Council. This Labour Council would also exercise control over the general activities of the trade unions, especially in regard to the appointment of officials.

The salient point of Nationalist Party propaganda was the allegation that the government alliance comprising the United, Labour and Dominion Parties, elected in 1943 to see the war through, was so concerned about fighting " England's war " that the needs of the South African people had been neglected.

Besides blaming the other parties for the shortages, discomforts and difficulties arising from the war effort, the Nationalists accused them of pampering the non-whites. They called them " Kafferboeties " (= Kaffir brothers, i.e. brothers, i.e. negrophiles) and said they were doing everything for the non-whites and nothing for the whites. They were contemptuous of the measures taken by the Smuts Government to maintain white supremacy and promised to enforce segregation in all spheres; to halt the flow of Africans to the urban areas; to keep the non-whites in their place; and to protect white workers from non-white competition.

The Nationalists won the 1948 general election and have remained in power ever since. As events have shown, it was not necessary for them to set up the precise machinery they advocated while in opposition. They have been able to achieve their aims, and much more besides, in various other ways. In its twenty years of rule, the Broederbond-inspired, " Christian-Nationalist " party has resolutely applied its apartheid policy, through numerous changes in the law, new enactments and regulations, and psychological and other pressures upon workers and employers.

3. Taming the Unions

On October 1, 1948 a seven-member Industrial Legislation Commission of Inquiry was set up to enquire into the four labour laws mainly affecting white workers and their unions and to make recommendations regarding wage fixing, the settlement of disputes, the control of trade unions and their affairs (including race separation), and " protection for all races " in wage regulating legislation.

The Commission was also directed to report on African trade unions and make recommendations upon suitable machinery for settling disputes between African workers and their employers.

Of the two white trade unionists on the Commission, one was a strong supporter of the government and the other died before the Commission's report was published. The report, which was submitted in December 1951, supported the government policy of state interference in the internal affairs of the unions and separate racial trade unions. It recommended conditional recognition of African trade unions, on a separate basis to that applicable to other races.

On the question of " protection of workers of all races " (i.e. racial quotas in employment, job reservation, etc.) the Commission could make no recommendation, explaining that this was a matter which should be entrusted to an expert scientific body.

From this 343-page report the government selected what it needed from time to time to put trade unions under restraint and to apply its race policies in the areas of employment and labour organisation.

Special action was taken against the Garment Workers' Union which, under the leadership of Mr. E. S. Sachs, had resisted frequent attempts by Broederbond-Nationalist groups to take over the organisation. The majority of the members of the union were Afrikaner women and the pretext for the attempts to overthrow the leadership was that Afrikaners had to be saved from " un-Afrikaans ", " un-national ", " un-Christian ", " alien ", " communistic ", influences.

On September 16, 1948 the Garment Workers' Union held a general meeting in the Johannesburg City Hall to discuss the terms of a new wage agreement. About 3,000 members attended The proceedings were interrupted by a rowdy mob which stormed into the hall. Fighting broke out and the meeting ended in disorder. The Union telegraphed the Minister of Labour, Mr. B. J. Schoeman, asking him to take action against the disrupters.

Instead, Mr. Schoeman set up a Commission of Inquiry to investigate not only the disturbances but also " the affairs and administration of the Garment Workers' Union ". The Commission sat for almost a year and finally reported on September 24, 1949. It was unable to provide the government with the desired excuse for direct intervention to oust Mr. Sachs and his colleagues.

But the government had another way of liquidating its opponents in the trade union movement. The first major blow at the trade union movement was struck with the passing of the Suppression of Communism Act in 1950.[5] This law conferred despotic powers upon the Minister of Justice, enabling him to deem persons to be communists, and order them to resign from their trade unions. It also gave him the power to prohibit persons from attending gatherings and this power was eventually widened so that trade union leaders and members were not only banned from attending gatherings of any kind, but, in addition, forbidden to enter trade union premises, factories and other places requisite to their functions.

The Minister used these powers to oust many able and experienced trade union leaders from their jobs, to make it easier for pro-government or docile aspirants to take over. Although these ends were not always attained, the unions were often disorganised and their bargaining power seriously weakened. By the end of 1955 no less than 56 key trade union officials, including Sachs, had been removed from office by Ministerial decree.

In 1954, the Minister of Labour produced a massive Bill to amend the Industrial Conciliation Act. It prohibited the formation of new racially mixed trade unions; compelled existing mixed unions to segregate their members in racial sections; prohibited racially mixed trade union meetings; excluded coloured members from mixed union executives; and empowered the Minister to reserve jobs on a racial basis.

Since its establishment in 1908, the mainstay of the South African Labour Party had been its trade union affiliates. Under the new law, it would be illegal for the unions to continue this affiliation or to give financial assistance to any political party or any election candidates. The white unions made a forlorn show of resistance to this grave interference in their affairs but were unable to arouse their apathetic rank and file, most of whom saw nothing wrong in what the government was doing. The few non-white and racially -mixed unions which tried to rally a massive demonstration against the Bill were unable to get the support of the powerful major unions.

The Bill was finally enacted in 1956, with only minor changes. Thereafter there was a significant retreat from militancy by the registered trade unions. Conscious of the minister's power to reject collective bargaining agreements, most unions took care not to offend the government. Those who attempted to hold the line were soon made to feel the pressures of authority. For example, the Minister refused to approve agreements which included May Day as a paid holiday and insisted upon the substitution of any other day, preferably May 31, which is now Republic Day. In this way the government was able to demonstrate to workers who was master, for May Day had been a workers' holiday (including post office, railway and other government employees) for over a quarter of a century.

To the Nationalist Party, however, it was " foreign ", " communistic " and " anti-South African " and had to be abolished.

4. Subjugating the Africans

The Nationalist government had least difficulty in subjugating African workers. This was largely because most whites feared competition from Africans or agreed that Africans were inferiors who needed to be disciplined, or felt that the fate of Africans was not their concern.

While other sections of the population waited apprehensively to see what the new government would do to them, the Broederbond masterminds, headed by Dr. Verwoerd, busied themselves in preparing plans for the greater control of the African majority. The maze of laws and regulations which afflicted the lives of urban Africans was steadily enlarged and their severity increased.

Only a few white trade unions protested in 1948 when the government abolished the payment of unemployment benefits to Africans. In the thoughtful mood of the post war days, the Smuts government had been persuaded to extend, for the first time, the contributory unemployment insurance scheme to African workers.

The new Nationalist government amended the Act within months of taking office to exclude all Africans earning less than £3.10.0d. a week. As at least 90 per cent of African workers fell into this category, the change amounted virtually to a total denial of benefits to jobless Africans.

In 1951 the Native Building Workers Act was passed, fixing a separate and inferior status for African building workers. They were prohibited from performing skilled work anywhere except in African areas or on white farms. To differentiate between them and white building artisans, a shorter training period and lower standards of skill were fixed, and they were placed on a far lower wage scale.

The absolute exclusion of African workers from collective bargaining was made law in 1953 in the Native Labour (Settlement of Disputes) Act, which prohibited white and Coloured unions from having African members and provided separate procedures for the settlement of disputes between African workers and their employers. African trade unions were denied official recognition and status and all strikes by Africans were prohibited under severe penalities.

Of far greater significance were the numerous other laws devised in this period by the Nationalists to enforce the " white master—black servant " system. Measures were taken to tighten control over the movement of Africans; to direct their labour; to ensure their obedience; to establish their impermanent urban status; and to subordinate them to the authority of government-appointed tribal chiefs.

In the twenty years of Broederbond-Nationalist rule, a mass of new and amending " Bantu " laws have been placed on the Statute book, all of which create a society in which the African majority is pegged to poverty and servitude.

Urban Africans are now far less secure than they were at the end of the war.

5. The Apartheid Plan

To lend respectability to their discriminatory policy, Dr. Verwoerd and his fellow Broederbonders conceived the ingenious plan of " separate development ". This conveyed to sensitive South Africans and the outside world that blue prints were being drawn for the partition of South Africa into separate, independent white and non-white territories, where the segregated people would have a separate but equal chance of economic progress and social justice.

As the twenty years have shown, this is humbug—a device to conceal the real intention of keeping the Africans in subservience for as long as humanly possible.

Dr. Verwoerd's plan had three parts, viz:

(1) effective action to reduce the number of Africans in the so-called " white " areas, i.e. the urban and industrial areas;

(2) measures for the economic development of the African reserves to provide a livelihood for Africans away from the " white " areas;

(3) the establishment of white-owned and controlled industries on the borders of the African reserves, for the employment of tribal Africans.

The first part of the Verwoerd plan has been and is being pursued with vigour. The government has shown itself to be quite ruthless in removing Africans from the towns to the desolate tribal areas.

The measures for the economic development of the African reserves—the 13.7 per cent of the country which is now being referred to as the Bantu homelands—are worth examining.

In 1950, the Tomlinson Commission was appointed to investigate " the socio-economic development of the Bantu areas ". In its report, dated October 1, 1954, the Commission recommended the spending of £60-million over a ten-year period for the development of secondary and tertiary industries. It estimated that the whites would have to spend at least £100-million in the following ten years if the policy of separate development was to have any chance of success. It pointed out that at least 50,000 jobs would have to be found every year for Africans living in the reserves. Of these new jobs, 20,000 would be in secondary industry. In a White Paper, the government rejected these targets, and stated :—

> *" The Bantu must start on a small scale. Psychologically, he is not adapted to industrial life and certainly not to private enterprise to be able to start on a big scale. It is only when he spends his own money, with moderate assistance . . . that he has an opportunity of adapting himself psychologically to the demands of industrial life ".*

Dr. Verwoerd was disappointed but not deterred by the findings of the Commission. His policy was that the poverty-stricken African people should pull themselves up by their own bootstraps. He would not even permit them to receive assistance from white entrepreneurs and financiers. He argued that if he allowed white South Africans and foreigners to provide capital for development, it would give them power in the Bantu homelands akin to colonialism. Instead, he set up a Bantu Investment Corporation in 1959 to mobilise African financial resources for the promotion of industrial and other undertakings.

From then until March 1968, a period of nine years, the Corporation gave assistance to only 16 minor industrial establishments, which provide work for a mere 614 Africans.[6]

On the basis of the Tomlinson estimate, at least 180,000 factory jobs should have been provided in the nine years.

If the Transkei (the first of the eight Bantustans) is any guide, the rate of economic development of the reserves is far from encouraging. No fewer than 278,000 Africans have to find employment outside the territory, there being only 32,700 jobs in the Transkei, apart from those filled by teachers, officials and subsistence farmers.

The third part of the Verwoerd plan is the border industry scheme. According to Verwoerd, white-owned industries on the perimeter of the African reserves would be able to make full use of African labour without creating social problems in the white areas or hampering the application of apartheid. Africans who work in border factories commute from townships inside the Bantustan, so that they work in a white area and live in a black area. From the time the border industry plan was instituted, border factories have provided jobs for only 189,541 Africans, according to a government estimate—which is probably optimistic, because several of the factories have moved from other areas and have not created new jobs. It is also significant that to make use of these 189,541 Africans, the factories have had to staff their establishments with 32,063 whites and 24,632 Coloureds. In other words, the border industries are drawing more whites and Coloureds closer to the African areas.

The Industrial Development Corporation (IDC), a government body, has been responsible for the establishment of most of the border factories through direct investment, loans to and partnerships with private investors. In its 1968 report the Corporation stated that from 1971, at least R80-million* must be invested annually in the border industries if work is to be provided for Africans in or near the Bantustans.

The signs are that nothing like this amount will be available in the foreseeable future, judging from the progress made thus far. By the end of 1967 the total capital investment amounted to only R295.5-million, of which R53-million had been provided by the Industrial Development Corporation.[7]

In its practical application the border industry plan is far different from what everyone imagined at the time Verwoerd expounded the theory. He gave the impression of factories going up in remote rural areas along the boundaries of the large reserves.

It turned out, however, that what Verwoerd had in mind was the 276 separate areas, many quite small and scattered within the "white" areas, which make up the eight Bantustans. On this basis, border industrial develop-

*South Africa used British currency values (£. s. d.) until February 1961, when a decimal system of Rands and Cents was adopted, one Rand being the equivalent of ten shillings sterling or 1.40 U.S. Dollars. Since British devaluation in November 1967, the exchange rate of the Rand has been 11s. 8d.

ment is taking place in the vicinity of long-established white towns and the curious situation has been created in which Pretoria is a " border area " but nearby Johannesburg is not; in which East London qualifies but Port Elizabeth does not.

Other white towns which fall into the border industry category are Durban, Newcastle, Ladysmith, and Rustenburg.

This means that in reality, they are extensions of existing metropolitan areas and if successfully developed, will be no different from such industrial areas as Johannesburg, Vereeniging and Port Elizabeth, excepting that all Africans working in the border factories will be migrants, while some of those working in the existing urban areas may still be able to cling to the diminishing right of domicile there.

The failure of the Verwoerd separate development plan is not only evident in the meagre development of the Bantu homelands and the paucity of jobs provided by the border industries; it is most marked in the continued increase in the urban African population. Verwoerd claimed that the measures he was taking would slow down the increase in the number of Africans in the urban areas, and by 1978 the trend would reach a turning point. From then onwards there would be a decrease and by the year 2000 A.D. the number would be back to the 1950 level—2,300,000. His optimism was not shared by the Tomlinson Commission which estimated that if the 1946–1951 tempo of urbanisation continued, there would be more than 10,000,000 urban Africans by the end of the century; and unless the absorbent capacity of the rural areas was considerably increased, there could well be more than 15,000,000 in towns outside the African areas.

The government is now faced with the stark reality that from 1946 to 1960 the urban African population almost doubled, from 1,800,000 to 3,400,000. By 1970 it is likely to be well in excess of 4,000,000.

At this rate, some six to eight million Africans will have to be expatriated from the urban areas to the wretchedly under-developed reserves to attain Verwoerd's 2000 A.D. target of 2,300,000. In a desperate effort to fulfil the Verwoerd plan, the government is now resorting to heartless action, regardless of the effect on African family life. Among other things it is forcing the old, the ill and the crippled out of the towns to distant " resettlement areas ", where amenities are few and employment non-existent. The unemployed, and those unable to work are no longer allowed to remain in the towns under the care of friends or families. They are " endorsed out "—that is, ordered to leave the urban area and go to a designated re-settlement area, far from family and friends.

In the five months from November 1967 to March 1968, more than 7,000 Africans were removed from Johannesburg alone.

The latest official move is to reduce all African workers, including those in industry and commerce, to the status of migrants, making their employment subject to the permission of a tribal labour authority and approved on a yearly basis only.

These measures are dealt with in Part Two.

The pattern of labour and racial legislation in South Africa today makes it abundantly clear that two decades of Broederbond-Nationalist rule have been calamitous for most of the country's workers. Even the measures which have been designed to pamper the privileged whites will in the long run recoil to their disadvantage.

Part Two

The Workers

1. Race Classification.

South Africa's labour force comprises workers of four race groups—Africans, whites, Coloureds and Asians. Race classification is determined in accordance with the Population Registration Act (Act. No. 30 of 1950), which sets out a rigid system of identification according to race.

This Act was the Nationalist Party's way of satisfying the popular demand among its followers for stricter laws to stop non-whites from " passing " as whites. Following the practice of the British colonies of the Cape and Natal and the Boer republics of Orange Free State and Transvaal, South Africa incorporated race definitions in many of its laws from Union in 1910 onwards. It was alleged, however, that because of inconsistencies in these laws, the desired racial distinctions were not being applied in many cases.

The Population Registration Act defines three main racial groups—" white ", " Coloured " and " native " (or " Bantu "). The " Coloured " group has seven sub-divisions, viz. Cape Coloured, Cape Malay, Griqua, Chinese, Indian, " other Asiatic " and " other Coloured ".

The general practice is to distinguish between the people in four categories—white, Coloured, Bantu and Asiatic—the Coloureds being mainly the people of mixed blood and the Asiatic mostly Indians.

The Bantu group is sub-divided into eight " national units ". The " homelands " of these eight ethnic units comprise some 276 separate areas. African identity cards state in which of the eight units the bearer has been classified: at the 1960 Census the size of each unit was given as follows:—

Xhosa	3,045,000
Zulu	2,867,000
Swazi	334,000
North-Sotho	971,000
South-Sotho	1,283,000
Tswana	1,149,000
Shangaan	511,000
Venda	246,000

Strict tests are applied to ensure that no one crosses the colour lines laid down by the government. A person is classified as " white " only if both his natural parents have been classified white. He is classified as " Coloured " if both his parents are in that category, or if one of his parents is white and the other Coloured or African. He is classified as " Bantu " if both his parents have been classified as " Bantu ".

In cases where one parent is African and the other Coloured the child is deemed to be " Bantu ".

The race label put on a non-white child at birth is not only the badge of race; it is a permanent brand of inferiority, the brand of class distinction. Throughout his life his race label will warn all concerned which doors are open to him and which are closed. In addition to the political and social taboos attached to his race identity card, it will proclaim what sort of education he may receive and the limits on his choice of employment.

If he is classified as " Coloured " he will be excluded from certain occupations reserved for whites; his trade union rights will be inferior to those of his white fellow workers; in many occupations his pay is likely to be lower. If he is classified as a " Bantu " he is in every way made inferior both to whites and Coloureds—in employment, earnings, trade union rights and everything else connected with making a living.

2. The Race Groups.

The population of South Africa, by race, is given in Table I below:—

TABLE I—Total Population 1960

	1960 Census	1967 Estimate
Africans	10,927,922	12,750,000
Whites	3,080,159	3,563,000
Coloureds	1,509,053	1,859,000
Asians	477,047	561,000

Source: Bulletin of Statistics. Vol. 2, No. 3, September 1968.

According to the 1960 census, 35.8 per cent of the whole population is economically active. The racial percentages are 37.4 per cent of whites, 36.7 per cent of Coloureds, 35.6 per cent of Africans and 26.4 per cent of Asians. The number of people in each of these four groups is shown in Table II:

TABLE II—Economically Active Population 1960

	Africans	Whites	Coloureds	Asians
Agriculture, Forestry & Fishing	1,438,835	119,312	120,258	10,847
Mining & Quarrying	548,317	61,748	4,489	595
Manufacturing	308,583	210,702	93,182	31,642
Construction	161,335	72,461	40,027	2,321
Electricity, Water, Gas & Sanitary services	25,905	10,488	2,918	285
Commerce & Finance	188,829	255,648	44,496	28,977
Transport, Storage & Communication	68,860	115,873	16,648	3,750
Services	821,152	260,281	144,774	23,492
Unspecified & presumably unemployed	328,196	44,538	87,147	23,949
	3,890,012	1,151,051	553,939	125,858

Source: Bulletin of Statistics Vol. 2, No. 2, June 1968.

As this book is largely concerned with people employed in industry, the number of employees in this sector of the economy are given in Tables III, IV, V and VI. These statistics are relevant to the labour laws, bargaining and trade union rights and wages of South Africa's workers, which are dealt with in later chapters.

Attention must be drawn to the fact that 90 per cent of the workers in the mining industry (Table III) are non-white, all but a handful being Africans.

In construction (Table V) Africans comprise 67.3 per cent of the labour force and whites only 19.2 per cent.

In manufacturing (Table IV) more than half the workers are Africans; one quarter are Coloureds and Indians and one quarter whites.

The extent to which South Africa depends upon non-whites and particularly Africans, for its industrial output and progress, is evident from Table VI, which lists the 19 main industrial groups and the number of workers of each race employed. Only in the printing and publishing industry are the whites in the majority, constituting a bare 55 per cent. In all other industries they are the minority, mostly a very small minority.

This fact is of utmost significance in evaluating the laws and practices which discriminate against non-whites on racial grounds in the fields of employment and trade union rights.

TABLE III—Employees in the Mining Industry

	1945		May 1968	
	No.	Percentage of total	No.	Percentage of total
Whites	51,564	11%	61,415	10%
Non Whites	421,466	89%	554,270	90%
	473,030	100%	615,685	100%

TABLE IV—Employees in Manufacturing Industry

	1945		1967	
	No.	Percentage of total	No.	Percentage of total
Africans	175,837	49.8%	530,000	52.6%
Whites	110,929	31.2%	254,400	25.3%
Coloureds	49,955	14.2%	163,600	16.2%
Asians	16,656	4.8%	59,100	5.9%
	353,377	100%	1,007,100	100%

Source: Statistical Year Book 1966—Bureau of Statistics.
Bulletin of Statistics. Vol. 2, No. 3, September 1968.

TABLE V—Employees in the Construction Industry

	1945 No.	1945 Percentage of total	1967 No.	1967 Percentage of total
Africans	21,692	64.2%	169,700	67.3%
Whites	8,502	25.2%	48,500	19.2%
Coloureds	3,539	10.5%	31,200	12.3%
Asians	57	0.1%	2,600	1.2%
	33,790	100%	252,000	100%

Source: *Statistical Year Book 1966 —Bureau of Statistics*
Bulletin of Statistics Vol. 2. No. 3 September 1968.

TABLE VI—Employees in Separate Industries—1967

	Whites No.	Non Whites No.	Non White percentage of total
Non-Metalliferous mineral products	14,200	66,200	94.0%
Metal Products	33,400	86,800	72.2%
Basic Metal	25,600	37,200	59.2%
Machinery	24,000	29,600	55.2%
Electrical Machinery	15,800	19,900	55.8%
Transport Equipment	24,700	39,500	61.5%
Clothing	10,800	83,400	88.5%
Textiles	7,800	65,000	78.5%
Food	19,900	99,400	83.3%
Chemicals and Chemical Products	18,200	38,900	68.1%
Wood and Cork	4,300	40,800	88.3%
Footwear	3,300	26,800	89.0%
Furniture	5,500	22,200	80.0%
Paper and Paper Products	7,400	21,900	74.7%
Printing	15,800	12,600	44.3%
Beverages	4,700	13,400	74.0%
Rubber and Rubber Products	4,700	12,700	73.0%
Leather and Leather Products	800	5,600	87.1%
Tobacco	1,500	2,800	65.0%

Source: *Bulletin of Statistics. Vol. 2, No. 2, June 1968.*

3. The Apartheid Base.

Like most of South Africa's other legislation, its labour laws discriminate between whites and non-whites, to the disadvantage of the non-whites.

In order to comprehend fully the extent of this discrimination, it is necessary first to consider the general pattern of apartheid as it affects workers. Apartheid, now referred to by the South African Government by the euphemism " separate development ", is applied through numerous laws regulating the political, educational, social and economic rights of the population.

By Act of Parliament in 1936, the whites decreed that 86.3 per cent of the country belonged to them and that the Africans would be apportioned the other 13.7 per cent, subject to conditions. No provision was made for the Coloured or Indian sections of the population.

On the basis of the 1967 figures, Africans constitute about 68 per cent of the population and whites 19 per cent. In terms of South African law, Africans can have no rights anywhere in the 86.3 per cent of South Africa which has been deemed to be " white "—the parts which contain the rich diamond, gold and coal mines, the heavy and light industries, the commercial centres, the railheads, the harbours and other places of employment.

Politically, all power is vested in the white minority. Parliament is reserved for whites only. The 166-member House of Assembly is elected by the white fifth of the population. The other four-fifths, the Africans, Coloureds and Indians have no say in the election of the Parliament which makes the laws.

The Senate of 43 elected and 11 nominated members is also an all-white body.

The Prime Minister of South Africa, Mr. B. J. Vorster, made it absolutely clear that he has no intention of giving political rights to urban Africans when he spoke in Parliament on April 24, 1968. He said:—

> *" . . . They remain there because they cannot provide employment for themselves. But the fact that you employ those people, does not place you under any obligation to grant them political rights in your Parliament. Surely the fact that you work for a man does not give you the right to run his affairs? . . . It is true that there are Blacks working for us. They will continue to work for us for generations, in spite of the ideal we have to separate them completely . . .*
>
> *The fact of the matter is this; we need them, because they work for us, but, after all, we pay them for their work . . . But the fact that they work for us can never . . . entitle them to claim political rights. Not now, nor in the future . . . under no circumstances can we grant them those political rights in our own territory, neither now nor ever ".*

It is essential to appreciate from the outset, therefore, that the vast majority of South Africa's workers have no political influence over the lawmakers and have no means, short of violent revolution, of changing the government.

Education is provided on a racial basis. The Department of Bantu Education, under the Minister of Bantu Affairs, controls the education of Africans. When Verwoerd, as Minister of Native Affairs, introduced his plan to apply apartheid to African education, he said the Bantu schools would equip Africans to meet the demands which the economic life of South Africa would impose on them.[1]

The Minister of Bantu Education said in June 1959[2] that because of the different environment of whites and Africans, " what one teaches them must differ ".

In the social sphere numerous laws give effect to the policy of apartheid. The Group Areas Act provides for the segregation of the people in separate residential and territorial areas. Segregation is also applied in transport. Where separate trains or buses are not provided, non-whites must use only the separate seats reserved for them. Stations, post offices and other public places have separate entrances for whites and non-whites. Separate days are set apart for white and non-white visitors to art galleries, museums, public gardens, zoos and libraries. Apartheid is applied to ambulance services, hospitals, clinics, health centres.

4. Urban African Workers.

Any examination of South Africa's labour laws and policies must be made in the light of the status of Africans in the urban areas. More than 4,000,000 Africans live in the urban areas. In spite of measures to limit the flow of Africans into the towns, the urban African population doubled between 1945 and 1960, when 3,471,233 were counted in the census. For twelve of those remarkable fifteen years, the Nationalist government was busily engaged in applying its policy of keeping the races apart.

For better appreciation of the situation, one should study the racial composition of the 13 principal urban areas, listed in Table VII. These centres of industrial and commercial activity have been designated "white" areas, although their white population is far less than their non-white. The greatest concentration of industry is on the Witwatersrand, where there are twice as many non-whites as whites and Africans alone outnumber whites by over half-a-million.

TABLE VII—Population of Principal Urban Areas 1960

	Africans	Whites	Coloureds	Asians
Johannesburg	650,912	413,153	59,467	28,993
Rest of Witwatersrand*	645,574	353,226	18,667	10,922
Vereeniging	52,424	24,564	1,024	823
Vanderbylpark	19,232	21,916	181	86
O.F.S. Goldfields	121,677	47,589	511	None
Cape Town	75,200	305,155	417,881	8,975
Durban	221,535	196,398	27,082	236,477
Pretoria	199,890	207,202	7,452	8,046
Port Elizabeth	123,183	94,931	68,332	4,247
Bloemfontein	75,944	63,046	6,281	2
Pietermaritzburg	55,991	40,065	5,715	26,827
East London	56,603	49,295	8,431	1,727
Uitenhage	21,519	17,531	9,309	396
	2,319,684	1,834,071	630,333	327,521

* Alberton, Benoni, Boksburg, Brakpan, Germiston, Krugersdorp, Nigel, Randfontein, Roodepoort, Springs.

Source: Statistical Year Book 1966.

These figures are a key to the real purpose of apartheid—the exploitation of non-white labour. Since soon after the first white settlers arrived in 1652, the belief has persisted that non-whites were ordained to serve the whites. This belief made it easier for fortune-seekers and entrepreneurs to extract the maximum of effort for the minimum of pay from their African labourers. With the discovery of diamonds and gold and the coming of industry, employers were always at an advantage over their employees because of the country's racial attitudes.

As the towns developed, the whites wanted African servants but resented having them in their midst. As the flow of Africans into the towns increased, new measures were taken to preserve the white master—black servant relationship. These measures increasingly diminished the rights of Africans. It was made clear by law and custom that non-whites were no more than sojourners in the towns and would be allowed to remain only by the grace of the whites and under stringent conditions.

The status of urban Africans was defined in 1921 by a Local Government Commission, which said:—

> *" The Native should only be allowed to enter the urban areas, which are essentially the white man's creation, when he is willing to enter and to minister to the needs of the white man, and should depart therefrom when he ceases so to minister ".*[3]

This attitude has prevailed ever since. It expresses the principle upon which all legislation affecting Africans has been devised. It is interesting to note that in 1921, the year of the Commission's postulate, there were only 658,000 Africans in the urban areas. This was 14 per cent of the total African population.[4] The white man's need for Africans to man factories and workshops, and " minister " to whites in their homes, offices, shops and other places, has been so great that by 1960, 31.8 per cent of Africans were urbanised. Regardless of all their harsh measures to control the influx of Africans into the so-called white areas, the whites have been careful not to deprive themselves of all the cheap black labour they want. This is evident from the statistics. On their part Africans have preferred to endure all the disabilities, injustices and hardships of discriminatory laws attached to urban employment, rather than the absolute poverty and hopelessness of the tribal areas.

5. Laws to Control Urban Africans.

The main laws which have been devised to control the lives and direct the labour of African workers are:—

The Bantu (Abolition of Passes and Co-ordination of Documents) Act. (Act. No. 67 of 1952)

The Bantu (Urban Areas) Act. (Act No. 25 of 1945)

The Bantu Administration Act. (Act No. 38 of 1927)

The Bantu Labour Act. (Act No. 67 of 1964)

The Master and Servant Laws.

(i) *The Pass Laws.*

The first pass law in South Africa was introduced by a British Governor of the Cape. The British seized the Cape in 1806 and on November 1, 1809 Earl Caledon issued a proclamation to provide Coloureds with " an encouragement for preferring entering the service of the inhabitants to leading an indolent life ".

Part of the encouragement was in the form of a prohibition against moving from district to district without a certificate issued by the landdrost. In various forms the pass system continued and expanded for generations until it became necessary for African townsmen to carry as many as a dozen documents of authorisation of one kind or another.

In 1952, Verwoerd brought in a new law which he magniloquently entitled Natives (Abolition of Passes and Co-Ordination of Documents) Act,* In spite of its title this law did not abolish passes; it actually extended the system to African women. In addition, it required every African to carry a reference book, containing his photograph, his race identity card, registered number, particulars of his tribal connections, his ethnic classification, the official authorisation to be in the urban area, his current tax receipt, the labour bureau permit to be employed or to seek work, the name, address and monthly signature of his employer, and various other particulars. Africans must always have their reference books with them. Failure to produce the book on demand by a policeman or other authorised persons results in immediate arrest. In the year ended June 30, 1966 there were 479,114 prosecutions under the pass laws, an average of 1,313 every day.[5] The Johannesburg average is 600 a day.[6] In the first nine months of 1968, more than 12,000 Africans were charged under various pass regulations in the Port Elizabeth Bantu Commissioner's Court.[7]

The onus is on the African employee to see that his employer signs his reference book every month. It is an offence not to have the current month's signature. Frequently Africans are arrested because of forgetfulness or their employer's lack of co-operation.

The Bantu (Abolition of Passes and Co-ordination of Documents) Act is perhaps the tightest permit control system in the world. It encourages whites to domineer in their relations with Africans and enables the government to discipline the African people and to direct African labour.

By compelling Africans to carry this reference book—really a packet of permits, a glorified pass—the authorities are able to enforce other racial laws. The pass system is the key to apartheid.

(ii) *Control of Movement of Africans*

The Bantu (Urban Areas) Consolidation Act (Act No. 25 of 1945) is the law which governs the entire existence of Africans in the towns. First applied in 1923, this Act has been revised, amended, and re-drawn on numerous occasions in desperate efforts to reconcile the conflict between racial prejudice and economic needs. With every stage of industrialisation and economic advance the authorities have been faced with increasing social problems, affecting all sections of the community, but particularly the Africans.

The purpose of the Urban Areas Act is to control the influx of Africans into the urban areas; to set apart areas for their accommodation; to direct their

---

*Now the Bantu (Abolition of Passes and Co-ordination of Documents) Act. All laws which originally referred to Africans as " Natives " have had this changed to " Bantu ". The Nationalist government refused to use the term " African " and even discarded " Native " in October 1958 by changing the title of the Department of Native Affairs into the Department of Bantu Administration and Development. Since then the official designation has been " Bantu ".

labour; and to impose strict regulations for their control and movement. In short, it aims at providing whites with black labour without allowing the blacks to acquire residential, social and other rights in the areas where they are employed.

The 4,000,000 Africans living in the urban areas are allowed to be there because they meet the qualifications laid down in the Urban Areas Act. However, these Africans do not acquire an abiding right of domicile by meeting these qualifications. It has now become abundantly clear that in practice an African is permitted to live in an urban area only as long as it suits white authority, regardless of his ability to meet the requirements of the law. The Bantu (Urban Areas) Act provides that no African is allowed to remain in an urban area for longer than 72 hours unless he or she is able to produce proof that:—

(a) he or she has since birth resided continuously in such area; or

(b) he or she has worked continuously in such area for one employer for not less than ten years; or has lived there with official permission for a continuous period of 15 years. (Those in this category must also prove that at no time in the periods mentioned have they been sentenced to a fine exceeding one hundred Rand* or to imprisonment for a period exceeding six months for any offence. They must also give proof that they are not employed outside that particular area); or

(c) she is the wife or unmarried daughter or that he is the son under the age of 18 years of a man who qualifies under paragraphs (a) or (b) and ordinarily resides with such person; or

(d) he or she has been given permission to remain in the area by a labour bureau official.

The full implications of the conditions placed upon residence in an urban area are contained in the meaning of "*such area*". In practice it means the area of one local authority. Consequently, it limits an African's right to residence and employment to one town. He is not free to take work in an adjoining town and set up home there, as whites do, nor can he work in one urban area and live in another as whites do. If he gets permission to enter employment in another urban area, from that in which he was born, he becomes a person in the category "specially authorised by the chief Bantu Affairs Commissioner" and his permit can be withdrawn at any time. Before he fully qualifies to remain in the town of his new job he must complete 10 years service with his new employer or manage to have his permit regularly renewed for the next 15 years.

No one is allowed to employ an African in an urban area without the permission of the local labour bureau. The employment of Africans is subject to the authority of the central labour bureau in Pretoria, which supervises and controls the numerous local bureaux.

Every African male over the age of 15 and under 65 must register at the local labour bureau within three days of becoming unemployed or within

---

*One Rand=ten shillings sterling or 1.40 U.S. Dollars. See footnote page 9.

14 days of reaching the age of 15. A labour officer endorses the African's reference book, *" Registered as a workseeker at the local labour bureau at . . . "*

Before the African can seek work, his reference book must bear the further endorsement *" Permitted to reside at . . . and to seek work as . . . within the prescribed area of . . . until . . . "*

In terms of Section 21*ter* of the Bantu Labour Regulation Act (Act No. 15 of 1911 as amended by the Bantu Laws Amendment Act of 1964), a district or municipal labour officer may refuse to sanction the employment of any African within the area of his jurisdiction if he believes " that such employment or continued employment impairs or is likely to impair the safety of the State or of the public or of a section thereof, or threatens or is likely to threaten the maintenance of public order ". If the African is already in employment, the labour officer can order his employer to dismiss him.

Once a ruling of this kind has been given by a labour officer the African is referred to an " aid centre " or to the district labour officer. (According to the government, the " aid centres " were designed to keep petty offenders out of jail; instead of locking up Africans arrested under influx control laws the police could take them to an " aid centre " to receive advice and help. By the middle of 1967 not a single " aid centre " had been established.)

The district labour officer can either offer the African employment elsewhere or " with due regard to the family ties or other obligations or commitments of such Bantu ", order him and his dependants to leave the area within a specified time. The chief Bantu Affairs Commissioner must confirm such orders in respect of Africans who were born in the area or who meet the 10 to 15 year residential and employment qualifications prescribed in the Urban Areas Act. The African may indicate to the labour officer the type of work he prefers and if satisfied as to the African's suitability, the labour officer notes on the record card that the bearer is eligible for employment in either manufacturing, mining, wholesale or retail trade, transport, domestic service or other specified class.

If the labour bureau is unable to place the African in employment immediately, his reference book is endorsed *" To report to the local labour bureau at . . . before . . ."*.

Within three days of giving an African a job, the employer must register a contract of employment with the labour bureau, and enter in the African's reference book his name and address and the date on which the African entered his service. The labour bureau then adds its own endorsement to the reference book, viz. *" Permitted to be in the prescribed area of . . . in terms of Section Ten (1) (a), (b) or (c) of Act 25 of 1945 and to be employed by . . . at . . . as . . . "*.

From the above it will be obvious that the pass system—the obligation to carry a reference book—plays a major part in the enforcement of the Urban Areas Act. It is also obvious that an African's right to residence in an urban area is linked with his job. If he loses his job he is in danger of losing his home.

If an out-of-work white man declines to accept a job on the grounds that it is not suitable the worst that can happen to him is the loss of unemployment benefits. For an African, however, it can have grave consequences. He may be treated as " idle " and dealt with in terms of Section 29 of the Act. This means he can be arrested without warrant and brought before a magistrate or Bantu Commissioner, who may declare him to be " idle " and order him to be removed from the urban area. In addition, the Commissioner may impose a permanent prohibition against the African returning to the urban area.

Under this Section of the Act an " idle person " includes an African—

(i) who has on three consecutive occasions refused or failed, without lawful cause, to accept suitable employment offered to him; or

(ii) who has more than twice within any period of six months failed to keep a job for longer than a month because of his misconduct, neglect, intemperance, or laziness; or

(iii) has on more than three occasions in one year been discharged from employment because of misconduct.

Urban Africans live under the constant threat of punitive action by the authorities if they become involved in strikes, demonstrations or public protests. Those who retaliate too vociferously or too vigorously against unjust treatment by their employers or rough handling by officials or policemen, are in danger of being expelled from their homes and sent to some rural area in the Bantu homelands.

Under Section 29, an African could always be declared to be an " undesirable person " if he had been convicted for certain specified crimes. In 1964 the government added a number of new ways in which an African could become " undesirable ". These additions were all politically motivated. Those convicted of offences under sections of the Riotous Assemblies Act, 1956, The Criminal Law Amendment Act, 1953, the Unlawful Organisations Act, 1960, and the General Law Amendment Act, 1962, thereafter fell into the category of undesirables.

The Riotous Assemblies Act was enacted in 1914 to prevent white workers from pressurising blacklegs and scabs in strikes on the gold mines and railways. It provided for the banning of meetings and the prohibition of publications and made it a crime to picket the homes or workplaces of the blacklegs and scabs or to annoy them or their families. This Act was amended in 1954 and consolidated as Act No. 17 of 1956.

The Criminal Law Amendment Act was enacted in 1953 to suppress the passive resistance campaign of defiance against unjust laws. It was made a crime to break any law as an act of protest or in support of any campaign against any law or for its repeal or modification.

The Unlawful Organisations Act was passed in 1960 to suppress the country's two African political parties, the African National Congress and the Pan Africanist Congress. It was made an offence to belong to any organisation declared to be unlawful or to further any of its aims.

The General Law Amendment Act of 1962 (Section 21) created the offence of sabotage, which it equated with treason. It defined sabotage as any wrongful or wilful act which " obstructs, injures, tampers with or destroys " the health or safety of the public; the maintenance of law and order; essential supplies or property; or attempting or conspiring to commit such acts; or in contravention of any law, being in possession of explosives, firearms or weapons, or entering or being upon any land or building.

Section 21 (2) throws the onus on the accused, after the prosecution has proved that he committed one of the several acts listed, that the act was not intended, among other things " to further or encourage the achievement of any political aim, including the bringing about of any social or economic change in the Republic ".

The Act excludes from this provision action taken by registered trade unions in terms of the Industrial Conciliation Act. As Africans are excluded by law from registered trade unions they are not protected by this exemption.

All this shows that there are many ways in which an African may find himself declared " undesirable " and then ordered out of the urban area, forfeiting his job and his residential rights. In terms of the 1964 law, he may be sent to a rural African village, settlement, rehabilitation scheme or institution.

The dependants of Africans ordered out of an urban area are also punished in terms of this law. They, too, are removed (at public expense) to join the unlucky breadwinner at the place to which he has been sent.

In 1966 the government embarked upon an intensified scheme for the removal of " surplus " Africans from the urban areas. The Minister of Planning, Dr. de Wet said on January 18, 1968 that the whole purpose of his Physical Planning and Utilisation of Resources Act of 1967 was " to decrease the number of Bantu labourers in the metropolitan areas ". This explanation came with a Proclamation freezing the African labour complements of 37 areas from January 19.[8]

The aged, the infirm, the chronically sick and those who cannot find work are being " endorsed out " of the urban areas and sent to " resettlement areas " in the African reserves. Apart from those in permanent employment, only the able-bodied, those capable of performing whatever labour is assigned to them, are likely to retain the right of urban residence. The over 40's who fall out of work through no fault of their own, are hardest hit because few employers will take on older men.

The Deputy Minister of Bantu Administration and Development, Mr. Coetzee, has vehemently declared that an African who does not work " must return to his homeland ". He said :—

> " . . . *must these people who are not employed or who are pensioners or who are living on charity or who are loafers be allowed to live in accommodation here which the taxpayer of South Africa has to provide and subsidize. Must they sit here because in terms of Section* 10 *they have qualified for the right to stay here ?* "[9]

Many of these victims have never seen the areas to which they are sent, even though the government calls these places their " homeland ". The fact that they qualified under Section 10 is evidence that they have not lived in a so called homeland for at least 10 or 15 years.

There are now some 30 " resettlement areas ", most of them consisting of a few shacks in the barren countryside. The only work available there is for a few able-bodied men on irrigation schemes. Absolutely no suitable employment is available for former factory and office workers.

The result is that transportation to a " resettlement area " usually means unemployment and poverty.

(iii) *Migrant Labour.*

The migratory labour system has been the basis of South African economic development. Lowly paid African migrant workers have been the greatest asset of the diamond and gold mining industries, and of the farming industry. They have also been a useful source of labour for industry, commerce and the services.

The migrants come from two sources—the African reserves and neighbouring territories. About 60 per cent of the Africans employed in South Africa's diamond, gold and coal mines are recruited on contract from Lesotho, Malawi, Rhodesia, Zambia, Botswana, Swaziland and Mozambique. African mineworkers are housed in compounds of single quarters, and not allowed to set up a home life with their families.

In addition to those employed on the mines, a large number of migrants are also employed on whites' farms and in the urban areas, under temporary permits.

The system began more than a century ago and from the beginning the whites have applied various pressures on Africans in the reserves to compel them to become migrant workers. The most successful measures were the hut tax and the head tax, which forced males to seek work where they could earn cash to pay their taxes. The migratory system has been severely condemned by expert commissions, medical experts, social workers and others, on the grounds that it is detrimental to the health of the workers, that it breaks up family life and that it creates numerous social and economic evils.

In spite of this, Dr. Verwoerd declared in 1955, when he was Minister of Native Affairs, that migratory labour was best for the mines and should be strengthened and expanded to serve most other spheres of labour.[10]

The Vorster government is now putting Dr. Verwoerd's suggestion into effect. As part of the apartheid plan, measures are being taken to shift the economy on to a migratory labour basis. On February 6, 1968, the deputy chairman of the Bantu Affairs Commission, Mr. Froneman, said in Parliament:-

> " *We are trying to introduce the migratory labour pattern as far as possible in every sphere. That is in fact the entire basis of our policy as far as the white economy is concerned, namely a system of migratory labour.*"[11]

On April 1, 1968, new regulations under the Bantu Administration Act came into operation, making it obligatory for every African, in or outside his tribal area, to register as a " workseeker " at a tribal labour bureau administered by his tribal chief.

In terms of the regulations, no African may leave his tribal area to work or seek work without the authority of the tribal bureaux, which will pool all " workseekers " in their respective areas, to provide labour as and when requisitioned by employers in the white areas. Employment is approved for a maximum period of one year or 360 shifts whichever is the shorter. At the end of that period, or as soon as a worker loses his job, he must return to the tribal area and remain there until his contract is renewed or another job is offered to him.[12] If his previous employer wants him back the employer must complete a " call-in " card, stating full details of the African's employment record, and his desire to return. The " call-in " card must also include a declaration that the African has been signed off and is not under obligation to work for any other employer. Obviously, this gives employers a powerful hold over their African employees, whose very existence may hinge upon the issue of a " call-in " card. The regulations also mean that all urban Africans who have not yet qualified for residence under the 10 or 15 year rule of Section 10, will never be able to do so. An African who has not completed 10 years' service with one employer or 15 years' service altogether, will now go into the tribal labour pool and be forced out of the urban area. As soon as an African loses his job and his right to remain in the urban area is challenged, an official can order him to go to a Bantustan, to register at the *tribal* labour bureau. From there he may be allotted work anywhere, including the urban area from which he was expelled.

If he has already set up a home in the urban area, he will have to give it up and take his family with him to the tribal area. Thereafter, he will see his family only when he returns from the urban area every year to await re-employment.

Employers in many industries who were concerned that the new regulations might create labour problems for them were re-assured by the Department of Bantu Administration and Development, which suggested that industrial groups should set up labour pools within the terms of the various laws, from which to draw their workers. It was suggested to the Johannesburg building industry, for example, that the employers form a registered labour supply company, which would be the legal employer of all African building workers in Johannesburg. Any African labour not available locally would be imported from the reserves and housed in compounds, as is done in the mining industry.

Under this scheme, migrant workers who were laid off, could be held in the pool instead of having to return to the tribal area.

From the African workers' point of view this may be worse than the migratory system. For one thing it opens the way for employers to replace settled urbanised workers reaching middle age by cheaper migrants, merely by increasing the migrant quota in the pool.

(iv) *Master and Servant Laws.*

Notwithstanding all the other means of disciplining African workers, South Africa still clings to her 19th century Master and Servant Laws, which were designed to ensure that African workers were unquestioningly obedient and respectful to their white masters. They apply mainly to domestic and agricultural workers.

Although the Master and Servant Laws make no distinction between white and non-white workers, they are invariably used to punish African workers who break their contracts of employment or misbehave. These contracts are rarely in writing and are assumed to have been made as soon as an African enters the service of an employer.

The Master and Servant Laws provide for criminal sanctions for breach of these civil contracts. It is a criminal offence for an African who has agreed to take a job not to do so; to desert or absent himself from work without lawful cause; to neglect to carry out his duties; to be unfit for work because of drink or drugs; to refuse to obey a lawful command or use abusive or insulting language to his employer or those in authority over him; or to take steps to change his job before the expiry of his contract. The average annual number of prosecutions for these offences is 22,000. In the year ended June 30, 1966 the number charged was 22,800.[13]

There are four Master and Servant Laws, one in respect of each of the four provinces. The Transvaal law dates back to 1880, the Natal to 1850, the Cape to 1856, and the Orange Free State to 1904. These are now incorporated in the Statutes of the Republic of South Africa.

Until the passing of the Native Labour (Settlement of Disputes) Act in 1953, the Master and Servant Laws were used to punish Africans who went on strike.

(v) *The Bantu Labour Act.*

The Bantu Labour Act (Act No. 67 of 1964) consolidates seven earlier laws regulating the recruitment, employment, accommodation, feeding and health conditions of African labourers in the mining industry.

Originally enacted in 1911 as the Native Labour Regulation Act, it includes provisions for the rigid control and discipline of tribal Africans recruited in the Bantustans and brought to work underground or elsewhere in the mines, under fixed contracts.

The penal sanctions of the Master and Servant Laws are repeated in Section 15 of the Bantu Labour Act.

Sections 21 and 22 provide for the establishment of the central labour bureau and the regional and district labour bureaux and for their powers and functions. A district or municipal labour officer appointed under these Sections has the power to refuse to allow any African to work within the area of his authority. He may order the African not to enter employment or to give up his job, if he is satisfied that the African is not qualified to be in the area, or that his employment or continued employment " impairs or is likely to impair the safety of the State or of the public or of a section of the public or threatens or is likely to threaten the maintenance of public order ".

(vi) *The Bantu Administration Act.*

The Bantu Administration Act (Act No. 38 of 1927) under which the regulations referred to above were proclaimed on March 29, 1968, was enacted in 1927 " to provide for the better control and management of native affairs ". It constitutes the President of the Republic of South Africa as the Supreme Chief of all Africans and empowers him to rule African areas by proclamation. The Act is based on a concept of native law formulated by white officials during British colonial rule. The President is vested with all the rights, powers, immunities and authority which were once vested in the British Governor of the colony of Natal. No court can pronounce on the validity of anything done by the President in his capacity as Supreme Chief.

The Bantu Administration Act empowers the President (i.e. the Minister of Bantu Administration and Development) to banish Africans to any place he decides. Between 1952 and 1964 about 130 Africans were banished from their home areas to distant places because of their opposition to the Bantu Authorities Act.*

One Section of this law was designed to deal with the Industrial and Commercial Workers' Union, one of the earliest African labour organisations, which had gained a large following throughout the country after the first World War. The Section sought to prevent "the dissemination of certain doctrines among the Natives" and made it a crime "to utter any words or do anything with the intent to promote any feeling of hostility between Natives and Europeans". It empowered magistrates to order the search of any premises and the seizure and confiscation of any leaflets, handbills, pamphlets, posters or papers which could be reasonably calculated to cause or promote such hostility. This was capable of wide interpretation, as any reference to racial discrimination could be deemed to arouse hostility among blacks or whites.

An example of this occurred in 1961, when the police seized and confiscated a quantity of pamphlets issued by the Non-European Railway Workers' Union on the grounds that they were calculated to cause or promote hostility, because they contained a complaint that white railway workers had received pay increases but non-whites had not.

The regulations gazetted on March 29, 1968 prohibit an African from leaving the area of his tribal labour bureau to take up employment without the authority of the bureau or an attesting officer. Generally, the regulations make it quite clear that this system of controlling the employment of tribal Africans is one of directing their labour to satisfy the needs of white employers and at the same time fit the apartheid schemes of a government obsessed with racialism.

*The Bantu Authorities Act (Act No. 68 of 1951) was devised to enforce the retrogression of Africans to tribal society. It provided for the establishment of tribal authorities and restored the declining power of chiefs, especially those who showed willingness to co-operate with the Government.

Part Three

Labour Laws

South Africa has a Ministry of Labour but the Department has only a minor interest in the affairs of African workers. As shown in previous chapters, the Department of Bantu Administration and Development controls the employment of Africans. The Department of Labour's responsibility is mainly confined to imposing upon Africans the legal sanctions of wage agreements made between white workers and employers, and to barring their way to certain jobs and keeping them out of registered unions.

The following laws are administered by the Department of Labour :—

Apprenticeship Act (Act No. 37 of 1944)
Bantu Building Workers Act (Act No. 27 of 1951)
Bantu Labour (Settlement of Disputes) Act (Act No. 48 of 1953)
Factories, Machinery and Building Works Act (Act No. 22 of 1941)
Industrial Conciliation Act (Act No. 28 of 1956)
Mines and Works Act (Act No. 27 of 1956)
Pneumoconiosis Act (Act No. 57 of 1956)
Shops and Offices Act (Act No. 75 of 1964)
Training of Artisans Act (Act No. 38 of 1951)
Unemployment Insurance Act (Act No. 53 of 1946)
Wage Act (Act No. 5 of 1957)
Workmen's Compensation Act (Act No. 30 of 1941)

The feature of most of these laws is the part they play in giving effect to racial discrimination. Besides laying down minimum standards of employment and treatment of workers and procedures for wage fixing and benefits, these laws also apply the policy of apartheid in employment and labour organisation.

1. Collective Bargaining.

The Industrial Conciliation Act gives legal effect to collective bargaining agreements between employers and their white and Coloured* employees.

It provides for the registration and regulation of trade unions and employers' organisations; for collective bargaining, arbitration and conciliation; and for job reservation.

In terms of this law, an African is not an " employee " and is therefore

*The Act defines a Coloured person as one " who is not a white person or a Native ", which means that persons of mixed blood, Indians and other Asians are classified as Coloured for the purposes of the Industrial Conciliation Act.

excluded from membership of trade unions registered under the Act and denied the right to participate in collective bargaining. This creates the curious situation in many industries that a white minority of workers do the bargaining and make the agreements with the employers, while the African majority, notwithstanding the fact that their wages and conditions form part of the agreements, have no right to argue their case. This unjust procedure is aggravated by the fact that the Minister of Labour gives legal force to the agreements and binds all Africans in the industries concerned to their provisions. This means the Africans are subject to the penal sanctions defined in the Act if they fail to comply with any provision or if they contravene any part of such agreements.

The extent of the injustice can be gauged from the following figures given in May 1964 by the Minister of Labour,[1] of registered agreements and awards.

	Number in force	*Workers Affected*			
		Whites	*Coloureds*	*Indians*	*Africans*
Industrial Council Agreements	131	150,082	91,268	27,037	284,148
Conciliation Board Agreements	5	562	629	8	1,142
Arbitration Award	1	641	13	93	2,432

As these figures show, of the 552,534 workers bound by the terms of the 131 collective bargaining agreements, more than half—the Africans—were prohibited from taking part in the negotiations with the employers. The racial composition of the labour force in the various industries (see Table VI) is a measure of the limitation of the principle of industrial democracy and is limited in South Africa. In all but the printing industry, whites are in the minority. Although some non-whites—the Coloureds and Indians—are qualified under the law to engage in collective bargaining, Africans are not. Yet they comprise nearly 90 per cent of the workers employed in mining, 52.6 per cent of those in manufacturing and 67.3 per cent in construction.

When employers and employees meet in industrial councils to negotiate agreements a member of the Bantu Labour Board—a white official—sits in on the discussions, watching the interests of the African employees who will be affected by the decisions. The attendance of this official is a farce. In the first place he has no mandate from the African workers, as he has not consulted them to ascertain their wishes. In any case, no democratic machinery is provided for him to obtain a collective viewpoint because, short of making African trade unions illegal the government does everything to destroy them and refuses to have dealings with them.

In the second place, the official is usually a man with little or no experience of collective bargaining or trade unionism or of the problems of the industries concerned. In the writer's experience the Bantu Board official was usually bewildered by the issues involved and appeared to think of Africans merely as menial labourers, and not as men performing tasks requiring skill and intelligence.

In a few industries, such as textile, clothing and leather, the registered unions have managed to maintain a liaison with the unregistered African unions. Before embarking upon collective bargaining sessions, the registered union meets the African union informally to decide upon the demands which will be put to the employer. In this way, the registered unions are able to present the claims of the unrepresented Africans as well as those of white and Coloured workers. This procedure involves risks for the registered union. Consultation with the Africans must be carefully arranged to avoid violations of the Industrial Conciliation Act.

The Industrial Legislation Commission admitted in 1951 that the interests of African workers suffered under statutory collective bargaining but the government has not thought it necessary to remedy the injustice. There are numerous examples of employers taking full advantage of the discriminatory bargaining system to exploit their African employees, while the white trade unionists have meekly acquiesced.

When employers are particularly stubborn on the question of wages for the top jobs held by whites, it is not surprising that the white negotiators abandon what little interest they might have shown in the pay for the jobs held by Africans.

One recent case where Africans suffered in this way was in 1968 in the engineering industry, where 75 per cent of the employees (about 190,000) are Africans. Six trade unions representing the 65000, white, Coloured and Indian workers in the industry, bargained with the employers for over six months before finally reaching agreement.

The unrecognised African Engineering Workers' Union could not take part because this is not allowed under the law. It submitted a memorandum, however, demanding higher wages and increased benefits; it asked for 26 to 27½ cents (2/7 to 2/9) an hour. All it got was what the employers offered at the outset, 19 to 22 cents (1/11 to 2/2½). Worse still, the agreement stipulated that Africans could not be employed in any of the top six categories of work, thereby applying a strict colour bar to employment in the industry. The wages in these six categories range from R1.00 to 81 cents (10/- to 8/1) per hour.[2]

2. The Wage Act.

When enacted in 1924 the Wage Act was intended as an alternative to collective bargaining, to protect all unorganised workers, including Africans. The Act gave all workers the right to obtain an investigation into their wages and working conditions by the Wage Board. The Board was obliged to make the investigation upon the request of any trade union, whether recognised by law or not, or where no trade union existed, upon the request of a representative number of employees.

In 1957 the government abolished this right and the law was changed so that the Wage Board could not act unless ordered to do so by the Minister of Labour. The procedure now is that if the Minister decides an investigation should be held, he tells the Board to do so and to report to him. After he receives their recommendation, he has the absolute right to decide its fate. If he approves a recommendation he publishes it in the Government Gazette as a Wage Determination applicable to the trade or industry specified, thereby binding employers and employees to its terms and conditions. The Minister can exempt individuals and classes of persons from the determinations.

There are several disadvantages in South Africa's Wage Board system, especially under the present race-obsessed government. In the first place the Minister is not particularly concerned about the wages of the voteless non-white workers, who most need wage protection. Secondly, the Wage Act is of no help to African workers employed in industries, trades and occupations covered by industrial council agreements. No wage investigation or determination can be made where collective bargaining agreements are in force. As explained above, such agreements are always extended to apply to Africans and, because of this, they are denied the right of remedy through the Wage Act.

A further weakness in the Wage Act is that it does not apply to agricultural and domestic workers, or State employees.

The Board, too, has limitations. It is restricted by the specific instruction in the Act that, before making a recommendation, it must take account of the ability of employers to pay higher wages and must consider representations from the Board of Trade and Industries, the Industrial Tribunal and any State Department.

The meagre benefits obtained by African workers through the Wage Act are evident from the wages provided in Wage Determinations. These are discussed in Chapter 9, together with the general question of wage discrimination.

The South African Government attempts to refute allegations of colour bias in wage fixing by drawing attention to Section 8(4) of the Wage Act, which provides that *"the Board shall not differentiate or discriminate on the basis of race or colour"*. However, the Act also provides in Section 5(b) that in making its reports to the Minister, the Board must show *"the class or classes of employees to whom it would be equitable . . . that remuneration should be paid at such rates as will enable them to support themselves in accordance with civilised standards of life"*.

In South Africa this means that whites must be paid more than non-whites, that a white needs a higher wage than an African because he lives on a "civilised standard" and the African does not.

It cannot be denied that the Board makes its recommendations to the Minister on the basis of the race of workers concerned. This is apparent from the wage rates they recommend for jobs performed by Africans, e.g. unskilled labour at R5 to R8.50 (50/- to 85/-) a week. In contrast, white labourers are never paid less than treble these rates.

3. The Right to Strike.

Under South African law, white and Coloured workers have a limited right to strike but Africans are denied the right absolutely.

Strikes by white and Coloured workers are governed by Section 65 of the Industrial Conciliation Act, which recognises their right to strike, except ng :—

(a) if they are employed by local authorities;

(b) if they are engaged in essential public services or utilities;

(c) while an industrial council agreement or a conciliation board or arbitration award is in operation;

(d) within one year after the publication of a Wage Determination covering them or their employers.

The Minister has the power to outlaw strikes by workers employed in the supply, distribution, processing, canning or preserving of any perishable foodstuffs or in the supply or distribution of petrol and other fuels to local authorities and essential services.

The Act also makes it illegal for a registered trade union to call or take part in a strike unless a majority of members in good standing have voted for such action.

For white and Coloured workers, the maximum penalty for striking illegally is £100 and one year's imprisonment.

In the case of African workers the maximum penalty is £500 and three years' imprisonment. The measure of this discrimination must be taken against the fact that Africans earn about one-fifth of the wages paid to whites.

The total prohibition of strikes by Africans is imposed by Section 18 of the Bantu Labour (Settlement of Disputes) Act, which states that *"no employee or other person shall instigate a strike or incite any employee or other person to take part in a strike or in the continuation of a strike"*.

In terms of this Section, a strike is defined extensively to cover stoppages, go-slows, refusals to work and similar action.

When, in spite of this harsh law and its ferocious penalty, Africans do go on strike, the authorities move in at once. One or more police vans, carrying armed police, rush to the scene to round up the strikers. If they refuse to resume work they are taken off to the police cells, to await prosecution. The Labour officials who intervene are usually quite unsympathetic and often bullying. They rarely try to dissuade the police from arresting the strikers and are careful not to offend the employers. It is not surprising that in most cases the African workers are forced to accept a settlement favourable to their employers.

A settlement, even when it shows the workers had good cause to strike, does not absolve them from punishment. The charge of illegal striking usually ends in the conviction of the strikers.

Besides the ferocious Settlement of Disputes Act, Africans have to beware of the danger of breaking other laws if they take strike action. They may fall foul of the Suppression of Communism Act and the Sabotage Act, with all their severe penalties. The Suppression of Communism Act includes in its definition of communism " *any doctrine or scheme which aims at bringing about any political, industrial, social or economic change within the Republic by the promotion of disturbance or disorder; by unlawful acts or omissions or by the threat of such acts or omissions or by means which include the promotion of disturbance or disorder, or such acts of omissions or threat* ".[3]

The Act specifically states that the President's power to declare an organisation unlawful cannot be applied to a trade union registered under the Industrial Conciliation Act, before the union has been given reasons and has appealed to the Minister of Labour.[4] The clear meaning of this is that African unions, not being registrable, have no such safeguard. It follows, therefore, that African workers' organisations can be declared unlawful without reason and without right of appeal. As it is unlawful for Africans to go on strike, such action could be deemed to be an " unlawful act " under the definition in the Suppression of Communism Act and the strikers liable, not only to prosecution in the courts but to arbitrary punishment by the Minister of Justice.

A classic example of the use of the Suppression of Communism Act against strikers is the case of the Port Elizabeth bus workers.* In January 1961, after negotiations with their employers had failed, 194 African bus conductors and drivers employed by the Bay Passenger Transport Company went on strike. They wanted the same wages and benefits as the white and Coloured employees of the Company and a minimum wage of £1 a day.

The 194 strikers were arrested and later released on bail. In support of their cause, the non-white bus users began a boycott of the buses. The effects of the dispute were felt far beyond the Company and its employees, so much so that the Mayor of Port Elizabeth called together the representatives of the workers and the Company to resolve the dispute. Both sides agreed to arbitration by an independent tribunal under the chairmanship of an ex-Chief Justice.

The tribunal awarded the workers increased wages, the same scale of bonus as white and Coloured employees and other benefits. This success offset in a degree the fines imposed on the 194 strikers—£7.10.0 each—after they had been convicted on the charge of striking illegally. It is revealing that the Company lent the strikers the money to pay the fines.

For ten of the strikers this was not the end. More than four years later, they were charged with furthering the aims of communism by taking part in the strike. In September 1965 they were convicted of belonging to the African National Congress (banned under the Suppression of Communism Act) and of furthering its aims by taking strike action in 1961. They were each sentenced to 4½ years' imprisonment. In August 1966, the Appeal Court reduced the sentences to one year.[5]

---

*This case was the subject of a complaint submitted to the International Labour Organisation by the World Federation of Trade Unions on March 14, 1966. As South Africa's membership of the ILO had formally ended three days earlier, the ILO referred the matter, with its recommendations, to the United Nations' Economic and Social Council. (See 91st Report of the Governing Body Committee on Freedom of Association, Case 472, July 1966).

On June 1, 1967 the UN Economic and Social Council referred the charges for further investigation and recommendations, to the *Ad hoc* Working Group of Experts set up by the Commission of Human Rights. (See Part Five).

The Sabotage Act[6] is another law which hovers over Africans who contemplate strike action. Section 21 (1) of this law provides that anyone will be guilty of sabotage if he commits any wrongful or wilful act whereby he obstructs, injures, tampers with or destroys the health or safety of the public; the maintenance of law and order; the supply of water, light, power, fuel or foodstuffs; sanitary, medical or fire extinguishing services; postal, telephone, telegraph or radio services; or the free movement of traffic; or any property.

To attempt, conspire or encourage others to commit any of these acts is also defined as sabotage. Sub Section (2) of the Act throws the onus on the accused to prove that the commission of any act falling within the definition (e.g. a strike) was not intended to achieve one of ten results, which include:—

> " to cripple or seriously prejudice any industry or undertaking . . . or the production or distribution of commodities or foodstuffs at any place; "
> " to further or encourage the achievement of any political aim, including the bringing about of any social or economic change within the Republic; "
> " to cause substantial financial loss to any person or to the State; "
> " to seriously interrupt the supply or distribution at any place of light, power, fuel or water, or of sanitary, medical or fire extinguishing services. "

As the ILO Committee on Freedom of Association has pointed out,[7] any strike whatsoever by African workers is a " wrongful act " according to the Settlement of Disputes Act. It would be extremely difficult for an African striker to prove that when he went on strike he did not intend to achieve any one of the several results set out in Section 21 (2).

It is significant that the Minister agreed, after representations from the Trade Union Council, to insert a proviso in the Act to exclude any act performed in relation to the Industrial Conciliation Act and the Railways and Harbours Service Act. This safeguard applies only to white and Coloured workers belonging to registered trade unions. African workers, because they are excluded from the provisions of the Industrial Conciliation Act, were left unprotected. They are, therefore, vulnerable to charges of sabotage and if convicted, liable to a minimum sentence of five years' imprisonment. The maximum is death.

It has always been argued by the South African Government that under its policy of separate development, Africans would be able to enjoy all the freedoms in their own areas, away from the whites. Part of the separate development plan is the border industry scheme, under which Africans live in their " homelands " and cross over the boundaries to work in white areas, in the white-owned factories just across the line.

The Minister of Labour has made it clear[8] that Africans working in the border factories* cannot have the right to strike and will be subject to the total ban on strikes in terms of the Settlement of Disputes Act.

---

*See pages 9 and 59.

4. The Bantu Labour (Settlement of Disputes) Act.

When the present South African Government party was in opposition, it frankly declared that it would never permit African workers to be treated equally with whites. Nationalist leaders promised the white electorate that it was their policy to maintain white supremacy and to " keep the kaffir in his place ". Today they are careful to use more diplomatic language but the policy is the same.

The Bantu Labour (Settlement of Disputes) Act was enacted in 1953 to end the growing trend towards a common labour code for all South Africa's workers. This law firmly shut the door in the face of industrialised Africans who were demanding the right to belong to registered trade unions and to engage in collective bargaining.

The Act is another of the many government devices to retard African progress towards equal status with whites. As with other such laws, it attempts to conceal the denial of rights behind a facade of a separate but adequate alternative. In place of collective bargaining it substitutes autocratic power in the hands of State officials, who are installed as spokesmen for African workers, without consultation at any level. These white officials are the government's substitute for trade union or workers' representatives. In any dispute between African employees and their employers, the complicated processes of the Settlement of Disputes Act come into operation.

As mentioned above, strikes are totally prohibited and punishable by a fine of up to £500 or three years' imprisonment or both the fine and imprisonment. This means that African workers cannot down tools or go slow or work to rule or use any of the usual means to gain satisfaction of their demands. Even strikes in protest against intolerable treatment, wrongful dismissal, bullying superiors and other injustices are not exempt from punishment. Workers cannot even strike against a change in the terms and conditions of their employment. In all circumstances, they must remain at work and wait for whatever settlement is reached between their employers and the white officials.

The Act provides that when a dispute arises, a Bantu Labour Officer (white) must report the matter to an Inspector (white) who in turn must inform a Regional Committee. This Committee comprises a white chairman and three African members appointed by the Minister. The Africans are not chosen in consultation with the African workers or any representative African body. The Minister selects men who go along with the government's apartheid policy, their knowledge of labour matters being a minor consideration. They usually stand in awe of the white officials and employers and lack the experience necessary to negotiate. Although Section 6(2) provides that a Regional Committee may receive " such representations from employees . . . as it may deem necessary " no provision is made to enable the employees to meet, formulate and present a common case, such as they would have as members of a trade union.

The Act also says that a Regional Committee must " maintain contact with employees " within its area, but in practice this rarely happens; when it does the contact is quite superficial and unhelpful.

If the Regional Committee cannot settle a dispute, it must refer the matter to the Central Bantu Labour Board, comprising a chairman and an unspecified number of white members, all appointed by the Minister. If the Board fails to reach a settlement, the dispute is passed to the Minister who may request the Wage Board to conduct an investigation and make recommendations.

After this long drawn out procedure, in which those directly concerned—the African employees—have not been allowed to take any direct part, the Minister settles the dispute himself by issuing an order, in accordance with the recommendations of the Wage Board. The terms of the order thereupon become binding upon employers and employees involved in the dispute.

There are certain provisions in the Settlement of Disputes Act which give the impression that Africans are not altogether excluded from voicing their grievances and demands. In practice, however, the provisions are hopelessly inadequate. For example, Section 7 provides for the election of Works Committees, consisting of not less than three and not more than five members, in establishments where there are 20 employees and more. This provision limits the combination of workers to the factory level, with all the obvious drawbacks. If evidence were needed to prove the Africans' aversion to this poor substitute for trade unionism, it can be found in the fact that 15 years after the passing of the Act, there were only 49 Works Committees in existence,[9] although there are probably some 20,000 factories, warehouses, garages and other establishments with more than 20 employees each.

This small number of Works Committees is additionally significant because of the strenuous efforts by the authorities to encourage their formation. On their part, employers look upon the committees as an instrument to ensure labour efficiency and discipline, rather than as a medium of free expression of workers' complaints and desires. In many establishments the committees comprise " boss boys " (African supervisors), and others favoured by the employer.

The Act also provides that whenever registered trade unions and employers' organisations negotiate agreements, the Bantu Labour Board must be advised, so that one of the Board members can attend to look after the interests of the Africans who will be affected by the agreement. The ludicrous inadequacy of this substitute for direct, organised African representation was demonstrated in the prolonged bargaining in the steel industry in 1968. The eight registered trade unions thought it necessary to have a team of 120 to represent the 75,000 white, Coloured and Indian workers in the numerous occupations covering the industry. In contrast, the 190,000 African operatives, assistants, labourers, storemen, general workers, etc., were represented by a government labour officer and a member of the Bantu Labour Board, for whom it must have been impossible either to consult the 190,000 Africans or to comprehend the complicated problems involved.

Although the government would like to show that the Settlement of Disputes Act is a satisfactory substitute for free collective bargaining, it is not distressed because of its failure. The main thing, as far as the government is concerned, is that Africans are being held in their inferior position and dare not strike for fear of the consequences.

5. Job Reservation.

The extent to which race prejudice has driven South Africa to fly in the face of economic realities is best illustrated in employment. The country pursues a policy designed to exclude non-whites from most jobs, yet without non-white labour South Africa's industry and trade would grind to a halt.

If Africans fell in with the apartheid policy tomorrow and prepared for a mass exodus to the undeveloped, inadequate reserves, the whites would be in a panic; the government would probably call out the police and the army to prevent them going.

As can be seen from Table VI, non-whites provide the greater part of the manpower in industry; in some industries they comprise 55 per cent of the labour force and in others 80 and even 90 per cent. Only in the printing industry do they amount to less than 50 per cent.

The colour bar in employment in South Africa has its origins in the early days of diamond and gold mining, when the mineowners made a determined effort to replace white miners by lower-paid Africans. Apart from the wage advantage, the mineowners were conscious of the fact that African employees, because of law and custom, would be docile and severely disciplined, in contrast to the militant whites, who constantly clamoured for more pay, shorter hours and other improvements.

The South African Republic under President Kruger had no sympathy for the mineowners' aims and thwarted their purpose by imposing a statutory colour bar in the mining industry. The alternative of giving workers protection from low-wage competition by means of statutory minimum wages and conditions of employment, was not even considered.

In 1893 the Transvaal Volksraad enacted a law prohibiting Africans, Asians and Coloureds from performing blasting operations—a major occupation in mining. In 1896 and 1897 further laws were passed reserving other mining jobs (work done by banksmen, onsetters and winding engine drivers) for qualified whites only.

When the British annexed the Transvaal in 1902 these laws were retained and after Union in 1910 the statutory colour bar in mining was embodied in the Mines and Works Act of 1911,[10] which empowered the Governor-General to make regulations for the issue of certificates of competency in skilled occupations in mining and engineering. Under these regulations, non-whites in the Transvaal and Orange Free State could not be granted certificates. In 1923 the courts declared the regulations *ultra vires* but in 1926 a new government (a Labour Party—Nationalist Party alliance) amended the law to reverse the court decision and restore the colour bar. Thereafter, certificates for engine driving, blasting, surveying and other skilled occupations in the mines were denied to Africans.

This was the only statutory colour bar until 1951, when the Nationalist government added a second, in the building industry. The Native Building Workers Act[11] of that year prohibited Africans from doing skilled building work in urban (i.e. white) areas. Their employment on such work was limited to African townships and reserves. To this end provision was made in the law for the training of African building workers for employment in such areas. This training period is a fraction of that for white apprentices, and the teaching limited to bare essentials. African building workers' wages are about one-third the rate for white artisans. In 1964 the minimum wage for a 45-hour week was fixed at R13.50 (£6.15.0) in the Cape; R12.75 (£6.7.6.) in the Transvaal; and R11 (£5.10.0) in Natal. The average minimum wage for white artisans was R31.99 (£15.19.11) in the Cape and R34.80 (£17.8.0) in Natal and the Transvaal, for a 40-hour week. African labourers, working under whites in the " white " areas were paid R9.88 (£4.18.10) a week in the Cape and R9.00 (£4.10.0) a week in the Transvaal.

The Bantu Building Workers Act also provided for the granting of certificates of competency to Africans who had acquired building skills by other means than the training courses, if they could pass a simple trade test. In the 15 years 1951–66, altogether 4,209 Africans were registered as Bantu building workers in terms of the Act.[12]

A wider application of the colour bar in employment was effected in 1956, by the addition of a new Section to the Industrial Conciliation Act, empowering the Minister of Labour to prohibit anyone from doing any job because of their race. The new Section 77, defined as " Safeguard against inter-racial competition " states that if the Minister thinks it advisable he may direct the Industrial Tribunal (a body of five government appointees) to investigate " any undertaking, industry, trade or occupation or class of work " and make a recommendation to him whether a colour bar should be applied and, if so, in what form.

The Minister may then issue an official determination, giving legal effect to the recommendation. A determination may:—

- prohibit the replacement of workers of one race by those of another race;
- compel employers to maintain a fixed percentage of workers of a particular race;
- reserve any class of work or specific jobs or work generally for members of a specified race;
- fix maximum, minimum or average numbers or percentages of persons of a specified race who may be employed in any factory, or industry or other places of employment.

The first industry to be investigated by the Tribunal was the clothing industry. After receiving the Tribunal's recommendation, the Minister decreed in October 1957 that from then onwards four main categories of work in the industry could be done by whites only. The jobs in question were at that date occupied by 4,500 whites and 35,000 non-whites. The Minister's determination may have seemed odd, especially as there was a shortage of white garment workers and it would have been impossible to replace a dozen, let alone 35,000 non-whites. However, the government had a deeper purpose. The immediate position was put right by mass exemptions, granted by the Minister, which allow employers to continue employing non-whites in the jobs reserved for whites, under permit.

This is the sinister element of Section 77. The Minister has the power to apply a colour bar to employment and then to grant and withdraw exemptions. In this way the State has taken power to direct labour at will and to intimidate employers. Wherever job reservation determinations have been applied, or are likely to be applied, employers as well as employees are at the mercy of the government. Exemptions are in the gift of the Minister, and it is not surprising that applicants are careful not to ruin their chances by showing themselves to be opposed to apartheid or the government.

Since the first job reservation determination in 1957, a further 23 have been made, and statutory race discrimination now applies to employment in the following industries and occupations:—

- Clothing industry
- Footwear industry
- Motor Assembly industry
- Building industry
- Liquor and Catering trade, Cape and Natal
- Motor vehicle driving, Durban, Orange Free State and Transvaal
- Barmen, Durban and Pietermaritzburg
- Passenger lift attendants, Johannesburg, Bloemfontein and Pretoria
- Traffic police, ambulance and fire services, Cape Town
- Road passenger transport, Cape
- Wholesale meat trade—abattoir section

According to the Minister of Labour, the number of workers potentially affected by these determinations is 105,000. He said he had granted exemptions to 513 individuals and general exemptions affecting 300 workers.[13]

The government defends job reservation as being " a positive method of promoting the orderly living together of the races " and claims that it is of benefit to the Coloured community " as only in that manner can they be protected against unfair competition from the Bantu ".

The Minister of Labour has attempted to substantiate this by issuing some determinations which reserve occupations for Coloured and Asian workers. Thus, Determination No. 15 reserves certain forms of motor driving in Durban for white, Coloured and Asian workers; Determination No. 16 reserves certain jobs in the motor vehicle assembly industry for white and Coloured workers; Determination No. 17 reserves some jobs in the liquor and catering trade in the Western Cape and Natal for Coloured and Asian workers; and Determinations No. 18 for the footwear industry provides that whites cannot be replaced by non-whites and Coloured workers cannot be replaced by Africans.

In this way the government is inculcating its racism into the minds of Coloured and Asian workers, making them believe that they need to be protected from Africans who are a threat to their employment and security. Most whites have always believed that the Coloureds should be made to feel that although they are several rungs below the whites, they stand much higher than the Africans. Fortunately, only a handful of Coloureds and Indians have responded to the government's temptation to support this deceptive, " divide and rule " racial discrimination.

(i) *Motor Assembly.*

On October 16, 1964 the Minister of Labour published Determination No. 16 applying racial quotas to employment in the motor assembly industry. Employers were ordered to maintain a minimum quota of white employees. The quota was fixed at 45 per cent for Bellville in the Cape, where the Chrysler plant was situated; and at Port Elizabeth where Ford and General Motors products are assembled, and at Uitenhage, 20 miles away, the Volkswagen and Studebaker plants were held to a white quota of 65 per cent. Assemblers on the Witwatersrand and in East London were given a smaller quota of 25 per cent, and Durban 20 per cent.

At that time, there were about 13,000 employees in the motor assembly industry, the racial composition being 52 per cent whites, 27 per cent Coloureds and 21 per cent Africans. Although the quota system favoured whites in the areas named, it encouraged employers to site their plants in the areas bordering the African reserves, where they would be immune from such labour restraints. In the years following the 1964 determination, there has been a trend towards the development of assembly plants in the border areas, as industrialists have taken advantage of the government's generous land, tax and other concessions to promote their border industry policy. By establishing themselves in the border areas, employers gained, in addition to all other benefits, the advantages of cheap, disciplined African labour and freedom from the quota system. Among the cars assembled at Rosslyn border area, near Pretoria, are Datsun, Rambler, Fiat, Alfa Romeo, Peugeot and Kaiser-Jeep. In the border area outside East London, Toyoto-Toyopet, Renault and Mercedes-Benz are assembled.

Although these makes represent less than 20 per cent of South Africa's total car production, they indicate the potential dangers in the government's border industry policy, especially in the competitive motor trade.

The big three in car production (Ford 21 per cent; General Motors 18 per cent; and Volkswagen 14 per cent) are under no illusions about the border industry threat and the quota system. Mr. R. J. Scott, managing director of the Ford Motor Company, said in 1967 that it was almost impossible to obtain white and Coloured workers and that the government's restrictions on the use of Africans was straining the Company's efforts to get workers.[14]

Coloured workers on the Port Elizabeth motor assembly lines also decided to look to their interests and formed a separate Coloured union in 1967, following a breakaway by whites from the former union. It was registered on

March 4, 1968 with 2,000 members as the National Union of Motor Assembly Workers.

The complications caused by job reservation and racial labour laws are leading to the fragmentation of the industrial council system, the basis of collective bargaining. An instance of this was the decision of Ford, General Motors and Volkswagen and their employees to break from the Industrial Council for the Motor Industry generally and apply to the government for separate registration as a council confined to the Port Elizabeth and Uitenhage plants.[15]

The motor assembly industry presents the government with a particular problem in the application of job reservation in the Pretoria area. Chrysler, whose share of the South African market is about 10 per cent, moved from the Cape in 1967 to a " white " area of Pretoria, some 10 miles from Rosslyn, the border area. On March 22, 1968, the Minister of Labour ordered the Industrial Tribunal to investigate the motor assembly industry in Pretoria to see if a job reservation determination should be made and if so, what form it should take. In accordance with the government's border industry policy, the Tribunal cannot recommend racial quotas at Rosslyn, so it would seem that the investigation is aimed at Chrysler alone. The pro-government, right wing white trade union, the Iron, Steel & Allied Industries Association, which has been enrolling white motor industry employees, has pressed for a determination for some time.

(ii) *The Engineering Colour Bar.*

In the engineering industry, where there had not previously been a statutory colour bar, employers and the registered trade unions signed a new agreement in 1968,* in terms of which Africans are excluded from employment in the top six categories. Section (1) of Part III of the agreement stipulates that " no employee shall be employed on work classified in this agreement at Rates A, AA, AB, B, C or D, unless he is eligible for membership of any trade union parties to this agreement ".

As Africans are barred by law from belonging to any of the unions, the stipulation is in fact an outright colour bar. The Minister of Labour cited this as a " voluntary application of the principle " of job reservation resulting from the existence of " watch dog " Section 77.[16]

Because the white trade unions and engineering employers have relieved the government of the task of applying a statutory colour bar under Section 77, the Minister has suspended two Determinations (Nos. 3 and 7) which previously applied to the industry.

Most of the unions who signed this colour bar agreement had been firm opponents of job reservation and their action was a capitulation to the government on the question of colour discrimination in employment. The first open declaration of support for Section 77 came on September 19, 1968 when Mr. T. P. Murray, general secretary of the South African Boilermakers'

---

*See page 30.

Society, announced that his union had officially applied to the Minister to apply job reservation to the engineering industry. He said the aim should be to "phase out" nearly 200,000 African engineering workers in the next 10 years and to limit their employment to the border areas.[17] He also suggested that the entire trade union movement should apply for a large number of selected jobs to be reserved for whites, Coloureds and Indians, except in border factories. The Minister of Labour, suspecting the motive behind the Boilermakers' proposal, dismissed it as "a clumsy attempt to discredit the government's labour policy".[18] The indisputable fact however, was that the government had received considerable new support from the trade unions for its policy of job reservation.

(iii) *The Printing Trade.*

One of the several ways in which a colour bar is applied in South Africa is through the demarcation of jobs. In other countries, demarcation decisions may affect the scope of a trade union or the tasks and pay of a worker. In South Africa a demarcation decision can exclude a man from a job because of his race. An example of this was a recent amendment to the main agreement in the Printing and Newspaper Industry,[19] which ruled that a "factory labourer" could not perform certain operations (standing at delivery end of a printing machine watching for rising spaces or type in the forme, or whether machine is printing correctly, etc., or do knocking up of printed sheets), as this was the work of a "general assistant".

Africans in the printing industry are confined to two categories—"factory labourer" and "unskilled labourer". By unwritten agreement with the South African Typographical Union, Africans are not employed in higher categories. Even though they acquire the simple skills, they cannot rise to become general assistants. The amendment quoted above is, therefore, a reservation of jobs for whites, Coloureds and Indians, to shut out Africans. The minimum wage of a general assistant is about R19.00 (£9.10.0) for a 40-hour week, while that of an African factory labourer is about R11.00 (£5.10.0) for a 44-hour week.

(iv) *The Case of the Indian Barmen.*

Unemployment among Natal Indians is chronic. Many depend upon the seasonal work available as waiters, barmen and assistants in Durban and coastal hotels. Most of the permanent barmen in hotels, bars and clubs are Indians. At the end of September 1968, the National Liquor Board issued new regulations forbidding the employment of Indians in bars where women are served.[20] Hoteliers complained that it was impossible to get white barmen and the secretary of the Natal Liquor and Catering Trade Employees Union said the regulations would hit a lot of its members, who would find it hard to get other jobs.

Apart from this action by the National Liquor Board, non-white barmen have been hit by two Determinations under Section 77.[21] These prohibit the engagement of a non-white barman to replace a white and reserve all future engagements and replacements for whites.

This discrimination against Indian barmen draws attention to the general plight of Indian workers, whose employment opportunities are further limited in other ways. The conventional colour bar applies to Indian applicants for jobs; should an employer decide to sign on an Indian apprentice, the white workers' representatives on the apprenticeship committee would promptly veto the application.

The Group Areas Act denies Indians access to jobs in many places and compels them to live in areas which are often all but inaccessible to their places of work.

Most of the half-million Indians in South Africa are descendants of workers brought from India from 1860 onwards to labour in the sugar canefields of Natal. Altogether 142,760 Indians were imported under indentured immigration.

In 1913 a law was enacted to stop further Indian immigration. Indians are not allowed to move from one province to another without official permission, which is granted only under exceptional circumstances. This makes it impossible for Indian workers to sell their labour on the best market or to seek jobs away from the areas of high unemployment.

About 82 per cent of the country's Indians are confined to Natal* which is unable to provide enough jobs for them. A 1961 survey by members of the University of Natal revealed that at that time 27.7 per cent of Durban's Indian working population was unemployed and seeking work.

One consequence of the job scarcity has tempted many Indians to seek a livelihood in commerce as small traders and about 21.8 per cent of the Indian working population is now believed to be engaged in commerce. This has provoked the Minister of Planning, Mr. Coetzee, to issue the following warning to the Indian community:—

> *"They must branch out into other occupations and become clerks, roadworkers and fitters and turners. I am sick and tired of seeing young Indians sitting on shop counters as if there were no other occupations open to them.*
>
> *Should they fail to do so willingly, I will be forced to take action. The day will come when we will have to reconsider the whole matter of trading licenses".*[22]

Mr. Coetzee did not explain what Indians should do to penetrate the barriers to employment erected in the conventional and statutory colour bars.

(v) *The Apprenticeship Colour Bar.*

The Apprenticeship Act (Act No. 37 of 1944) governs the registration and training of apprentices in skilled trades. It provides for the establishment of apprenticeship committees in each industry and on their advice the Minister of Labour prescribes the conditions of apprenticeship including minimum age, educational qualifications, period of training, technical classes to be attended, rates of pay and hours of work.

---

*The rest live in the Transvaal (13 per cent) and the Cape (4 per cent). No Indians are allowed to live in the Orange Free State.

The majority of apprentices are trained in five industries—building, engineering, motor, mining and printing, which altogether accommodate 90 per cent of all apprentices. During the five year period to December 31, 1967 a total of 44,660 apprenticeship contracts were registered, of which 40,254 were in respect of whites, 3,832 Coloureds and 574 Asians.[23] This ratio of one non-white (i.e. Coloured or Indian) apprentice to every ten whites has been fairly consistent for the past 50 years.

Although the law does not deny Africans the right to become apprentices, they are excluded by an established practice in all trades, whereby employers do not sign on African apprentices. The few Coloureds and Indians who have been able to enter into contracts of apprenticeship, are mostly concentrated in special areas: the Coloureds mainly in the building, motor and furniture industries in the Cape Peninsula and the Indians in the building, motor and engineering industries in Durban.

The rule to exclude non-whites generally, as well as Africans particularly, from training in the skilled trades, is strictly observed in all other areas. All apprenticeship contracts must be approved by the apprenticeship committees and the very few employers who have attempted to sign on non-whites have had such applications turned down.

The attitude of white artisans towards non-white apprentices is exemplified in the motor trade in the Cape and Natal, where white motor mechanics have refused to train Coloured and Indian apprentices. At a Parow (Cape) garage in March 1967, six white motor mechanics walked out when the owner engaged a Coloured apprentice to serve under a Coloured mechanic. The employer had to dismiss the apprentice to end the dispute.[24] In September 1968, the union of white motor mechanics, The Motor Industry Employees Union, (M.I.E.U.) ordered its members to stop training the non-whites, on pain of fines, suspension or expulsion from the union.[25] As the closed shop operates in the motor trade, such expulsion would be followed by exclusion from further employment in the trade.

An organiser of the Motor Industry Combined Workers' Union, the 5,000-strong union of Coloured and Indian workers in the motor industry, stated that matriculated Coloured youths had been shut out of the trade because the apprenticeship committee, " obviously influenced by the white union's representatives, turned down all the applications ".[26]

A similar situation arose in Durban, when the city's electrical engineer suggested the training of Africans as electricians to work in the African townships because white electricians were afraid to enter African residential areas after dark. White workers protested immediately. Their unions—the Amalgamated Engineering Union and the Electrical Workers' Association—held a protest meeting to demand that the Durban City Council drop the plan.[27]

(vi) *Apartheid for Nurses.*

A statutory colour bar was imposed on the nursing profession in 1957 by the Nursing Act[28] of that year, which forbids the employment of non-whites in posts where they would supervise or control white staff. This law also provides that only whites may be appointed or elected to the Nursing Council, the body which controls the profession. The Council is authorised to prescribe conditions and qualifications for entry into the profession on a racial basis.

(vii) *" Civilised Labour " policy.*

The so-called " civilised labour " policy is another colour bar in employment. It was first applied in 1924, when the Nationalist—Labour government of the day instructed state departments and provincial authorities to employ " civilised " labour instead of " uncivilised " labour, i.e. to employ whites and not Africans in unskilled jobs. The instruction defined " uncivilised labour " as " the labour rendered by persons whose aim is restricted to the bare requirements of the necessities of life as understood among barbarous and undeveloped people ".

With the rising demand for labour during and after the war, whites found better work and the " civilised labour " policy fell into disuse. However, in 1949, soon after being elected to power, the Nationalists instructed all state departments to restore the policy and within two years, 1,290 Africans had been replaced by whites. This revival was short-lived however. The continuing economic boom created such a labour shortage that even the State was forced to employ more Africans. By 1956, the government railways were employing 15,353 non-whites in jobs previously occupied by whites.

It has been made clear by the government that this is only a temporary arrangement. Whenever a white labourer wants a job with the government, he will get it, even if an African has to be thrown out to make way for him.

Like other government departments, the Post Office has always been a white preserve, with non-whites kept at a minimum and employed only in the menial jobs. At April 1968, the Post Office employed 34,788 whites and 13,671 non-whites. For years South Africa has suffered an acute shortage of postmen but rather than take the obvious course of abolishing the " white labour " policy for this kind of work, the government merely took on non-whites in a temporary capacity, with the warning that once whites became available, the non-whites would be replaced. At the end of February 1967 there were 1,835 non-white temporary postmen and messengers.[29]

Yet even this minimal relaxation was fiercely criticised by white employees. The South African Postal Association, the union of uniformed post office workers, declared in a resolution at its 1968 congress that " the appointment of non-whites as postmen will be opposed with all the power at our command ".[30]

(viii) *Manpower Shortage.*

The South African Government has been fortunate in being able to operate its apartheid policy during a period when economic circumstances have been all in its favour. The country's economy has been remarkably resilient to the pressures of job reservation and racial discrimination in employment. In spite of the brakes on productivity, output has continued to rise and foreign trade maintains an upward trend.

As far as the government is concerned, any slowdown in the economy is preferable to a sacrifice of even a small part of its race policy. It would rather suffer a continuing shortage of skilled and semi-skilled manpower than concede to non-whites the opportunity to acquire skills on equal terms with whites.

In October 1968, the South African Foreign Trade Association (Safto) stated that manufactured goods are unlikely to become a dominant factor in the country's export scene for many years, mainly because the industry is suffering from a shortage of skilled and semi-skilled labour.

(a) *Railways*

Because of a serious shortage of skilled whites, there has been a fairly widespread evasion of work reservation practices by management. Even the government has been compelled to employ Africans on jobs traditionally regarded as " white ". The Johannesburg *Star* reported on October 25, 1967 that the Railways Administration had brought teams of Africans into the Durban goods yards during the night hours, to carry out shunting operations. The Africans were officially classified and paid as shunters' mates.

In 1968, the Minister of Transport revealed how the employment pattern has changed on the railways and how the government is still struggling to maintain the colour bar, in face of economic necessity. Speaking of the acute shortage of white staff, he said:—[31]

> " . . . *I can solve the problem fairly easily by employing non-whites as firemen, driver's assistants . . . shunters, guards, station-foremen, artisans, etc., I can easily do so. But there would be tremendous opposition from the staff . . . I am already employing non-whites in work previously done by whites . . . I am employing Coloureds and Bantu as for example, ticket clerks, work previously done by whites. There are certain types of skilled work previously done by whites which are now being done by non-whites . . . At present there are seven or eight thousand Bantu who do the pick-and-shovel work on the permanent way which used to be done by whites. This is also the case as far as flagmen and pointsmen are concerned . . . There is tremendous opposition from the staff, and I back them up. In certain grades and posts one simply cannot use non-whites . . . One cannot use a Bantu as a fireman on an engine. This will simply not be tolerated. It cannot be done, because we cannot have a mixed working of whites and non-whites . . .* "

(b) *Mines*

In 1967 the mining companies persuaded the white miners to agree to some minor relaxation of the colour bar in return for increased wages and fringe benefits. A new productivity agreement gave the white employees an average wage increase of 11 per cent and allowed Africans to perform a few operations previously reserved for whites only.

But the white mineworkers and the government will resist any further relaxation of the colour bar in mining. At a public meeting at Evander,

Transvaal, on May 25, 1968, the Minister of Labour reiterated a previous assurance to the Mineworkers' Union that in border areas, *or even in African areas,* where mine development was taking place, only whites would be granted blasting certificates.[32] In another speech on November 23, 1968, at Kempton Park, Transvaal, the Minister took the matter further. He said it was unheard of to think the government would even consider any proposal to replace white miners with non-whites and he declared that as long as the Nationalist Party remained in power the white workers would be protected.[33]

(c) *Construction*

A continuing manpower shortage in the building industry from the 1950s onwards resulted in fierce competition for the available skilled white labour and drove employers to embark on an extensive recruiting campaign overseas. During the early 1960s white artisans were obtained from Mozambique, Portugal, Holland and other countries. In the year ended June 30, 1966, South Africa received 3,097 immigrant building artisans but in the following twelve months the inflow dropped to 2,591 and in the next nine months to March 1968 only 1,378 entered the country.

The manpower shortage is worsened by the difficulty in persuading white youths to become building trade apprentices. There is an intense dislike for this type of work, especially the wet trades, among whites. The shortage could be overcome, of course, by abolishing the colour bar and letting non-whites do the work. The opposition of white workers to this has been aggravated by the desire of employers to take advantage of non-whites by paying them lower wages, and thereby depressing wages generally.

Nevertheless, a minor breakthrough occurred in the Transvaal in February, 1966, when a productivity agreement permitted Africans to do preliminary paint work. In practice, Africans were doing even more than this, with the unions, employers and authorities turning a blind eye. Towards the end of 1968 the employers and registered trade unions had reached a new agreement which represented a significant departure from job reservation. African painting operatives were to be allowed to paint roofs, apply first coats of paint, strip down and clean paint surfaces; plastering operatives would smooth and take off excess plaster and do slushing; bricklaying operatives would do jointing, filling-in and smoothing mortar; and woodworking operatives would operate a wide range of machines under supervision.

This agreement must be approved by the Minister of Labour before it becomes legal. His decision was not known when this was written but he had agreed to similar deviations in the Cape, by way of an exemption from Job Reservation Determination No. 13, which permitted Coloureds to do work reserved for white operatives.[34]

The Electrical Workers' Association warned that it would resist any attempt to dilute or fragment electrical work in the building industry, to allow Africans to take over part of white artisans' work. The Association said: "Unless something is done to stop the rot that has set in, we are faced with the bleak prospect of white employees walking the streets looking for work".[35]

If the Minister agrees to the departures from the rule, he will do so only as a temporary expedient to help employers over the labour shortage and not to advance Africans. Should a recession hit the building industry, the concessions will be revoked and the African operatives replaced by whites, in accordance with government policy.

(ix) *Violating the ILO Convention.*

In June 1958, the International Labour Organisation adopted Convention 111[36] concerning discrimination in respect of employment and occupation, under which member states were asked to pursue and promote equality of opportunity and treatment for all inhabitants, with a view to eliminating discrimination.

The convention defined discrimination as any distinction, exclusion or preference made on the basis of race, colour, sex, religion, political opinion, national extraction or social origin, which could nullify or impair the right of equal opportunity or treatment in employment.

Needless to state, South Africa is not among the 63 nations which have ratified this convention. Discrimination forms the basis of South Africa's employment policy, and as shown in these pages, race discrimination is applied against non-whites :—

- by laws such as Section 77 of the Industrial Conciliation Act, the Mines and Works Act, the Bantu Building Workers Act and the Nursing Act;
- by provisions in collective bargaining agreements, which exclude Africans from occupations and are given lawful effect by the Minister (e.g. in engineering, printing, etc.);
- by convention—the unwritten, mutual understanding between employers and registered craft unions that no Africans—and as far as possible no Coloureds or Indians—should be apprenticed;
- by the State's " civilised labour " policy, giving preference to whites in the filling of all unskilled vacancies in government and provincial departments;
- by apartheid laws and regulations which prohibit racial mixing and thereby exclude non-whites from certain jobs (e.g. the case of the Indian barmen quoted above).

(x) *The Secret Weapon.*

It is being argued nowadays that the increasing encroachment of non-whites into occupations previously the preserve of whites is a clear sign that the colour bar in industry is breaking down. This is a superficial assessment of the changes that have taken place during the period of an acute shortage of skilled white labour.

Although more jobs have been made available to Africans, in most cases this has been done on a temporary basis and subject to the government's pleasure, and generally at wage rates which no white would accept.

In assessing the concessions that have been made, it is necessary to bear in mind the government's policy. When Section 77 was introduced in 1956, the then Minister of Labour, Senator de Klerk, emphasised that this was a mechanism to ensure white preference in times of unemployment. The Nationalists were determined that in the event of unemployment, the whites would not be in the queues, only the non-whites. If there had to be jobless, let it be the Africans, the Coloureds and the Indians but not the white voters. Senator de Klerk made this clear when he told Parliament, " now is the time to tackle this matter, because when a recession comes, we will have the weapon ".

The present Minister of Labour, Mr. Viljoen, re-affirmed this policy of white preference in times of unemployment in June 1968, when he said:—

> " *It is not being denied that during recent years a reclassification of certain types of employment has taken place . . . But what is important is that where a reclassification of types of employment has taken place, whether it was at Iscor*, or whether it was in the engineering industry, or in whatever facet of our economic or industrial life it took place, this change took place in the first instance with the consent of the white trade unions and white workers concerned. That reclassification was not forced upon these people against their will and desire. It was done in consultation with them. It was done with their consent. It was done on certain conditions, i.e. that if there should be any kind of economic recession, or something of that nature, that work which has at present been transferred to the non-whites would, if it should ever become necessary, be returned to the whites in that a reclassification can be made* ".[37]

The whole purpose of job reservation and its convenient exemptions is exposed in this cruel threat to conscientious, hard working non-white workers—they will be discarded when it suits white authority, not because of their incompetence or misbehaviour, but because of the colour of their skin.

6. Unemployment Insurance.

The 1946 Unemployment Insurance Act[38], was the first tentative move by the Smuts' government to accede to the view that Africans should be treated on the same basis as other workers. The Act provided for a contributory unemployment scheme, run by the State; it included Africans and other non-whites in commerce and industry. Those excluded fell in two main

---

*The Iron and Steel Corporation of South Africa—a public utility corporation established by Act of Parliament in 1928, in which the State holds a minimum of 51 per cent of the voting rights and nominates the majority of directors. Iscor provides iron and steel for South Africa's engineering and other industries.

categories (a) public servants, domestic, agricultural, seasonal and casual workers; (b) African mineworkers; Africans employed in rural areas, except in factories.

The exclusion of African mineworkers was at the insistence of the mining industry and of the rural African workers, to placate the farming industry.

The mineowners vehemently protested when the idea of unemployment insurance was mooted, declaring: " At a time when so many employers are in need of Native labour, it is illogical that large numbers of Natives should be able to draw unemployment benefits and live in idleness at the expense of the State ". At the time the mines were short of some 20,000 African underground workers; the pay was two shillings and eightpence a day, plus food and quarters, it being a requirement that all African employees " lived in " at the compounds provided near the shaftheads.

The 1946 Act was resented by most whites and particularly by employers. The Nationalist Party responded by extending its racial discrimination; soon after coming to power they changed the Act to exclude all Africans earning a basic wage of less than £182 a year.[39] As 90 per cent of African workers fell in this category, the change virtually amounted to total exclusion.

In 1957, the terms of the exclusion were re-phrased[40] to make it clear that only Africans whose total earnings, inclusive of cost-of-living and other allowances, amounted to more than £273 per annum (£5.3.3 a week) qualified as contributors to the Fund. Almost all wage determinations and industrial council agreements fix African wages below this qualifying rate, and consequently leave all but a few Africans without insurance. This means that when an African loses his job, he gets nothing while out of work.

Discrimination against African unemployed is even carried into official statistics. The Department of Labour, which keeps a record of the unemployed, takes no account of jobless Africans. South Africa's unemployment statistics apply only to whites, Coloureds and Indians. The unemployment figure published every month ignores the jobless among more than half the country's labour force in industry and commerce—the Africans.

Thus, in February 1967 (the last occasion when the government made this information available) there were 78,272 Africans out of work. But South Africa boasted to the world that she had only 14,922 jobless—6,810 whites and 8,112 non-whites—" less than two per cent, the recognised measure of full employment ".

African workers, employed and unemployed, fall more within the jurisdiction of the Department of Bantu Administration and Development than the Department of Labour. The Department of Bantu Administration and Development does not keep the same type of unemployment register as the Department of Labour. It is not interested in unemployment as a welfare problem, but simply as one of control and discipline of African workers.

Now that the government is stepping-up the removal of Africans from the urban areas, the loss of a job may lead to an African being banished to distant parts, far from the only place where he is likely to get a job.

7. Workmen's Compensation.

The Workmen's Compensation Act[41] is a State accident insurance scheme, under which employers are compelled to insure their employees against accident and industrial diseases. Workers injured at work or who contract disease arising from their work are entitled to receive medical treatment and compensation on scales defined in the Act.

The onus is on the employer to notify the Workmen's Compensation Commissioner of accidents and industrial diseases. In the case of Africans, the report must be made to an officer of the Department of Bantu Administration and Development.

This Act provides a grim example of the callous attitude of employers and the State towards African workers. Periodically, the Commissioner publishes a list of workers who have not claimed compensation due to them. At least three-quarters are Africans. The five lists published between December 1966 and August 1967, contained the names of 8,730 Africans to whom compensation had been awarded, but who could not be traced.[42]

One reason why the African claimants cannot be found is that employers do not bother to keep proper records of these employees. Although employers are obliged to note the National Identity Number of every African in their employ, this does not seem to have helped the Workmen's Compensation Commissioner or the Bantu Affairs Commissioner to trace injured Africans in the twelve-month period which precedes publication in the Government Gazette.

Until recently, many employers recorded only the first name of their African employees and a staff number (e.g. Jim No. 15), not bothering to note a surname, a home address, next of kin, or other necessary particulars.

A second reason is the migrant labour system. After being involved in an accident, migrant Africans return to their tribal homes, unable to await an award or unaware that they are entitled to compensation. They may have departed under orders in terms of influx control regulations, being "endorsed out" of the urban area on the loss of employment. Illiteracy, the lack of trade union protection, and unsympathetic officialdom are other factors which cause Africans to lose compensation money due to them.

8. Apartheid in Factories.

The Factories, Machinery and Building Works Act[43] provides for the registration and control of factories, the regulation of hours of work and conditions of employment in factories, the supervision of the use of machinery, precautions against accidents and related matters.

Sections of the Factories Act lay down maximum hours of work, sick leave, holidays and the payment of wages applicable to workers who are not protected by other wage regulating measures, i.e. industrial council and conciliation board agreements, wage determinations and awards.

The policy of apartheid is embodied in regulations under the Act, which require employers to provide separate rest and dining rooms, washing facilities, change rooms and toilets for whites and non-whites.

If the Minister is of the opinion that special provision is necessary in any factory " to safeguard the physical, moral or social welfare of employees ", he can order the factory owner to separate the races or sexes. To give effect to this order, the owner may be required to keep the races or sexes apart by partitioning work rooms.

9. Wage Discrimination.

In South Africa, wages are fixed in one of three ways—

(a) through procedures provided in the Industrial Conciliation Act (collective bargaining, conciliation or arbitration);

(b) by the Minister of Labour on recommendations by the Wage Board;

(c) by employers.

The workings of the Industrial Conciliation Act and the Wage Act have been described earlier. Whatever the method, Africans have no say in the matter.

(i) *Mineworkers.*

The prime example of what happens when employers are left to determine the wages of their employees, is the mining industry. Although the mining companies negotiate with their white employees through six registered trade unions, they alone decide what to pay their African employees. Not surprisingly, the average cash wage of the whites is seventeen times greater than that of the Africans, who comprise 90 per cent of the labour force in the industry.

The mineowners attempt to defend this vast difference by arguing that their African employees, in addition to cash wages, are housed and fed and given free medical treatment. The housing consists of walled-in compounds of single quarters only, with concrete bunks; the food is a standard diet to provide each worker with about 4,000 calories a day at a cost to the mineowners of about 17 cents (1s. 9d).

The compounds provide accommodation for males only; married men cannot live there with their wives and families; nor are they allowed by law to set up homes in places near their work, as these are defined as " white " areas.

From establishment at the end of the 19th Century, the mining industry has maintained this form of employment, recruiting migrant Africans from the reserves and all neighbouring states, on minimum contracts of 180 to 270 shifts. No government has attempted to interfere with this labour policy, in the conviction that this is the only basis upon which the country's gold, coal and diamond deposits can be profitably mined. Dr. Francis Wilson, lecturer in the Department of Economics of the University of Cape Town, investigated the wage structure of the gold mining industry and found that in real terms, the cash wages which Africans earn in the gold mines are no higher now and possibly even lower, than they were in 1911. He published two tables, which included the following comparisons:—[44]

	Average Annual Cash Earnings			
	White	Black	White	Black
	Current Rands*		1938 Rands*	
1911	665.8	57.0	850	72
1966	3,215.9	182.8	1,241	71

	Average Earnings per Shift			
	White	Black	White	Black
	Current Rands*		1938 Rands*	
1936	2.83	0.26	3.00	0.28
1966	11.70	0.77	4.52	0.30

(The Shift earnings are cash only for whites and cash plus food for blacks)

Dr. Wilson pointed out that the white/black earnings gap widened from 11.7 to 1 in 1911 to 17.6 to 1 in 1966.

It is worth recording that gold mining at deep levels is particularly hazardous and despite considerable precautions the accident rate is high. In 1966, mining accidents resulted in the death of 762 miners, and injury to 30,677. Most of these occurred in the gold mines of the Witwatersrand and Orange Free State, where 34 whites and 551 Africans were killed and 1,903 whites and 24,288 Africans injured—a fatality rate of 1.40 per 1,000 employees and a casualty rate of 63 per 1,000.

In the coal mines, where some 25,000 Africans are employed underground and another 11,000 on the surface, the degree of wage discrimination is even greater. The average monthly wage of white underground workers is R303 (£151-10-0) while that of Africans working alongside them is R15.47 (£7-14-9).[45] It is true that the Africans, in addition to their cash wages, get free board and lodging; but whites also get other benefits, such as cheap family housing. As in the gold mines, all but three per cent of the African workers must live in single quarters in closed compounds, separated from their families and females.

(ii) *Manufacturing Industry.*

In the manufacturing industry, where most workers are covered by industrial council agreements or wage determinations, Africans get a better deal than in mining, but their average wage is little more than one-fifth that of whites.

The gap between white and non-white earnings is in fact widening. Mr. Anthony Davenport drew attention to this in a special examination[46], in which he showed that in the ten-year period 1957-1967, the difference between

***One Rand=ten shillings sterling or 1.40 U.S. Dollars. See note on page 9.**

average white and African wages increased from R120 a month to R194 a month, viz:

	Average Monthly Wages		
	1957	1967	*Increase*
Whites	R146	R238	61.4%
Africans	R26	R44	59%

He pointed out that to prevent the actual wage gap from widening further the percentage of future pay increases for Africans would have to be five and a half times greater than that for whites. In other words, an increase of 10 per cent in white wages would need a 55 per cent increase in African wages to keep the gap at the R194 level.

The *Financial Mail,* Johannesburg[47] was able to show that the percentage increases have actually been smaller for Africans than for whites, viz:

	Average Monthly Wages		
	March 1962	*March* 1967	*Increase*
Whites	R161.73	R231.87	43%
Africans	R32.39	R43.22	33%

These increases take no account of the rise in living costs. The consumer price index, which is taken as the indicator of the cost of living (base 100 = 1958) had risen to 120.2 in March 1967.* The real wage increase in the ten-year period from 1957 to 1967, would therefore be no more than 35 per cent, if proper allowance is made for the lower purchasing power of money. In any case, comparisons on a percentage basis (which the government and its economist supporters seem to prefer) tend to blur the picture, because African wages have always been so low that even a 100 per cent increase on 1957 wages would not raise the level to what has been estimated to be a living wage.

This is borne out by several surveys of urban African incomes and expenditure, conducted in recent years. Table VIII quotes figures of African family incomes and minimum essential expenditure given in the four main surveys, which have been accepted as a reliable guide.

TABLE VIII—Incomes and Expenditure of Urban African Families

Survey	Year	Area	No. of Wage Earners per Household	Size of Family	Average Family Income	Minimum essential household expenditure	Monthly Shortfall
de Gruchy[1]	1958	Johannesburg	1.3	5	R39	R48.32	R9.32
Suttner[2]	1966	Johannesburg	1.3	5	R46.31	R55.57	R9.26
N.E.A.D.[3]	1967	Johannesburg	(a)	5	(a)	R53.32	R12.57
BMR[4]	1967	Port Elizabeth	1.9	5.4	R59.16	R63.89	R4.73
		Uitenhage	1.9	5.4	R58.01	R63.89	R5.88

*By December 1968 it had risen to 125.9.

(a) The Non-European Affairs Department calculated on one earner per family, on which basis there was a shortfall of R12.57. It stated that 67.6 per cent of the families covered by the Survey had incomes below the poverty datum line.

1 *Cost of Living for Urban Africans* Johannesburg 1959 by Joy de Gruchy, Institute of Race Relations, Johannesburg, 1960.

2 *Cost of Living in Soweto*, by Sheila Suttner, Institute of Race Relations, Johannesburg, 1967.

3 Johannesburg City Council, Non-European Affairs Department, 1967.

4 Bureau of Market Research, 1967.

Note: The amounts in last three columns are in South African currency—rands and cents. One rand=ten shillings sterling or 1.40 U.S. Dollars.
See footnote on page 9.

TABLE IX—Wage Determinations:—February–September 1968

Wages fixed for labourers, general workers, and for two lowest grades.

Determination No.	Date	Industry	Job*	Weekly Wage
295	16/2/68	Manufacture of Soap, Candles, Edible oils or Fats.	(c) V	R8.20
			(c) IV	R8.60
296	22/3/68	Dairy (Witwatersrand & Pretoria)	delivery employee	R8.60
			(a)	R8.00 (plus 50 cents p.w. in lieu of lodging.)
297	19/4/68	Clothing (Border Areas)	(b)	R5.35
			(b) qualified	R7.25
			(a)	R4.70 to R5.70
298	30/5/68	Manufacture of Ladies Stockings	(c) II	R8.75
			(c) III	R7.75
			(a)	R5.75
299	16/8/68	Bread & Confectionery (East London, King Williams town and Queenstown)	(c) I	R7.13
			(a)	R6.67
300	23/8/68	Hairdressing (East London, Bloemfontein, Welkom etc.)	(a)	R7.00
301	30/8/68	Condensed Milk & other Milk products (Bethal, Standerton, Volksrust, Estcourt etc.)	(c) I	R8.97
			(c) II	R8.51
			(c) III	R6.67
			(c) IV	R5.75
			(a)	R5.52
302	20/9/68	Commercial Distributive Trade	(b) Johannesburg	R10.25
			Country Towns	R8.20
			(c) I	R11.60
				R9.55
			(c) II	R10.85
				R8.80
303	27/9/68	Transport Undertaking (Goods)	(a) Towns	R9.00
			(a) Country	R5.75

Note: 1. In column four, letters refer to (a) labourers; (b) general workers; (c) workers in two lowest grades.
2. Wage determinations remain in force indefinitely.
3. Wages are in South African currency—rands and cents. One rand = ten shillings sterling or 1.40 U.S. Dollars. (See Note on page 9).

Privation compels mothers and often children to take on jobs over long hours to supplement the family income. The African townships abound in delinquency because of both parents going out to work and there being few and in some areas no creches and generally inadequate school accommodation. The absolute poverty of families with only one wage earner can be seen everywhere. No matter how hard an African works, how zealous his service to his employer, he is rarely rewarded adequately. That is evident from the figures quoted from the surveys. If further evidence of this exploitation were necessary, one only need look at the minimum wages still being fixed for jobs occupied by Africans, in wage determinations and collective bargaining agreements. The statutory minimum wage rates in the nine wage determinations published between February and September 1968, for labourers, general workers and, where applicable, to the next two lowest grades are given in Table IX. It should be mentioned that many of these workers perform semi-skilled tasks in production, as operatives or in repetitive jobs requiring special ability.

In seven of the determinations the Minister has promulgated wages ranging from as little as R5.75 a week (R24.92 a month) to no more than R9 (R39 a month). In one, which applies to the clothing industry in areas bordering the African reserves, employers are authorised to pay unskilled workers R4.70 to R5.70 (R20.37 to R24.70 a month).

The best deal is in the commercial distributive trade, where the rate for labourers in Johannesburg is R10.85 (R47.02 a month). Even this is well below the poverty datum line given in Table VIII.

In the industrial council agreements, there are a few instances of better treatment, but the general pattern of poverty wages for Africans is the same. Table X consists of fourteen industrial council agreements published in the same eight-month period, February to September, 1968.

This table shows quite clearly that the top wage for jobs normally occupied by Africans is being held at around R9 to R11 a week (R39 to R47 a month) but in some industries and trades the rate ranges from R6.35 to R8.75 (R27.50 to R38 a month).

(iii) *Employers' Ability to Pay.*

An interesting aspect of the African wage pattern in South Africa is that Ministers, employers, registered unions and others agree (and have been saying so for at least twenty years) that African wages should be lifted above the poverty level. Yet improvements are rare and when made, are small and too far behind price rises to be of much help. Employers are particularly guilty of humbug on the issue. According to the findings of the Johannesburg *Business Times* " Barometer of Business Opinion " conducted by Market Research Africa, no less than 85 per cent of leading businessmen declared that a major national effort should be made to raise the average wage of African workers.[48] It has become a habit for employers to talk in this way, yet to do nothing.

As far back as 1957 leading members of the Johannesburg Chamber of Commerce set up a special body styled The Bantu Wage and Productivity

TABLE X—Industrial Council Agreements:—February–September 1968

Wages fixed for labourers, general workers and for two lowest grades.

Date	Industry	Period of Agreement	Job*	Weekly Wage
8.3.68	Baking and Confectionery (Cape)	2 years	(a)	R9.00
			(c) delivery employee	R9.00
28.6.68	Baking and Confectionery (Durban & district)	2 years	(c) III	R9.00
19.7.68	Building (Durban)	3 years	(a) I	R9.46
			(a) II	R10.75
5.4.68	Building (Northern Natal)	3 years	(a)	R5.06 plus 28 cents holiday pay
			(a) Grade I	R6.21 plus 35 cents holiday pay
15.3.68	Chemical (Cape)	2 years	(a)	R9.00
			(c) I	R11.00
26.4.68	Clothing (Eastern Province)	2 years	(a)	R10.50
			(b)	R9.00
3.5.68	Clothing (Natal)	3 years	(a)	R9.25 } Durban
			(c) II	R9.25 } Durban
			(a)	R8.33 } Pietermaritz-burg
			(c) II	R8.33 } Pietermaritz-burg
22.3.68	Cotton Textile Manufacturing (Cape)	to 31/12/69	(c) II	R8.74
			(c) III	R8.51
13.9.68	Electrical (Natal)	2 years	(b) Rate 9	R10.35
			(b) Rate 10	R9.22½
			(b) Rate 11	R8.55
3.5.68	Furniture Manufacturing (Orange Free State)	3 years	(a)	R7.70
19.4.68	Iron, Steel, Engineering and Metallurgical (South Africa)	2 years	(b) Rate G	R8.55
			(c) Rate H	R9.90
14.6.68	Wholesale Meat Trade (Witwatersrand)	5 years	(a)	R7.75
23.2.68	Sweetmaking (Cape)	3 years	(c) II	R9.30
			(c) III	R8.50 (Plus service allowance 25 cents after 5 years, 50 cents after 10 years)
12.7.68	Sweet Manufacturing (Port Elizabeth)	1 year	(a)	R8.75
			(b)	R10.50

Notes. 1. Column four—(a) labourers; (b) general workers; (c) workers in two lowest grades.
2. Wages are in South African currency—rands and cents. One rand = ten shillings sterling or 1.40 U.S. Dollars. (See Note on page 9).

Association, to see what could be done to raise African productivity and wages. Eleven years later an ex-president of the Association stated: " By and large I feel that wages are at a realistic level related to the present contribution of workers in industry ".[49] He was referring, of course, to poverty wages such as those listed in Tables IX and X. But he added a revealing rider: " Too many firms, however, have fixed wages at the minimum statutory level. In a number of cases an increase of between R2 and R3 a week will not significantly push up costs or lead to dangerous inflationary tendencies ". Increases of this order would mean, in many cases, pay rises of as much as 40 per cent.

Industry's ability to pay African workers more cannot be in doubt. Net profits are moving continually upwards. The *Financial Mail,* Johannesburg has compared the profits of 1961–62 with those of 1965–66,[50] to show that in the earlier period the total net profits of 248 listed companies amounted to R78.3-million compared with R150-million for 224 listed companies in the later period.

The extent to which wage increases fail to bring African incomes within reach of living costs was well illustrated in the case of Port Elizabeth municipal employees, who were given pay rises in May 1968. Before the rises, unskilled workers were paid R7.95 and semi-skilled from R8.31 to R12.45; thereafter unskilled rates were R9.10 and semi-skilled from R9.46 to R13.80. These earnings were supplemented by an incentive bonus, which made it possible for unskilled workers to earn R10.10 per week and semi-skilled workers from R10.46 to R14.80.

This still left all but a handful of the municipal workers well below the poverty datum line. As shown in Table VIII, the minumum essential expenditure of an African household has been calculated as R63.89 per month or R14.75 per week.

And, as so often happens to the poorest workers, even the little was to be taken away: the pay rises were to be swallowed up by rent increases. The Port Elizabeth City Council told ratepayers that the wage increases would be " more than sufficient " to cover the rent increases to be imposed in the African townships.[51]

(iv) *Government Resistance.*

The South African Government has made no effort to persuade employers to pay their African employees a living wage. On the contrary, the authorities have discouraged progressive employers from setting an example. The Minister of Labour, Mr. Marais Viljoen made his racial approach to the question quite clear when he was Deputy Minister; he declared on May 21, 1959 :—

> *" To plead that you must pay the Natives who are employees a ' civilised wage ' means only one thing in this country—white wages.*
>
> *To want to pay Natives white wages fails in the first place to take account of their productivity, in the second place it does not take their living standard into account ".*

This spells out the provision in the Wage Act which requires the Wage Board to state the " class " (i.e. race) of workers for whom it recommends " remuneration . . . in accordance with civilized standards of life ".

This is the basis upon which the Minister acts as pacemaker in wage fixing. In defence of this discrimination in remuneration, the government hides behind the mummery of the Bantu Labour (Settlement of Disputes) Act and claims that the Bantu Labour Board has succeeded in getting wage increases for Africans to the extent of R47-million in nine years. This globular, almost a magic figure has never been proven. Possibly the Bantu Labour Board is taking credit for all the pay rises for all Africans since 1958, which is absurd, because it has had little or no influence in bringing about improvements, such as they are.

In any case the proof of the pudding is in the actual wages paid. These demonstrate, without doubt, that most Africans are considerably underpaid.

(v) *Stake of Foreign Investors.*

The heartless exploitation of non-white workers in South Africa is not entirely a domestic matter. Foreign investors, too, are profiting from the country's cheap black labour policy.

British, European and American manufacturers who have establishments in South Africa, are swelling their profits by being able to pay their African employees as little as one-fifth the rate payable for the same work in their own countries.

Overseas manufacturers whose goods are made under licence in South Africa also derive benefit from such low wages. Workers in British, French, German, Italian, Dutch, United States and Canadian factories would be shocked if they knew what Africans are paid for doing the same work for their employers in South Africa.

(vi) *Border Industries.*

Differential wages are also applied to Africans on a regional basis, in factories bordering on African reserves. The establishment of these factories has been promoted by the government as part of its plan to draw off Africans from the urban areas.*

Apart from numerous other benefits, entrepreneurs are enticed to the border areas by the cheap, disciplined labour force made available by the government.

The prevention of labour organisation or trade union activity in these areas is an important factor in keeping wages down.

Employers are usually left to pay their African employees whatever they please. Where national wage determinations or collective bargaining agreements previously included the border areas, the government was quick to step in to have the rates adjusted to suit its cheap labour policy. One example of this is the clothing industry. A machinist in the border area of Hammersdale (between Durban and Pietermaritzburg) is entitled to a minimum wage of R10.50 a week, compared with the legal minimum of R15.00 in Durban, 27 miles away, or R17.73 in Port Elizabeth and East London. General workers in a Hammarsdale clothing factory get a wage of R6.75, in Durban R9.25 and in Port Elizabeth and East London R10.50.

The Minister of Labour has also authorised lower wages than the statutory minimum for workers in the textile, motor, engineering and canvas goods factories in the border areas. In six instances the Minister's decision superseded collective bargaining agreements. Although, as required by law, he consulted the industrial councils concerned, they had no choice in the matter; whatever they say the Minister has the overriding power to do what he wants.

Replying to complaints that the low wage policy in the border industries endangers the employment of higher-paid workers in the urban areas, the

---

*This is described in Part One.

Minister has given the assurance that it will not be applied " in such a way that it prejudices the employment position of the white workers in any white area ".[52] He made no mention of the African, Coloured and Indian workers in the urban areas, who are mainly affected by cheap wage competition from the border areas.

Wages in these areas are likely to remain low not only because the employees, being Africans, are denied trade union access to collective bargaining, but because jobs are scarce, opportunities almost non-existent, and the freedom to seek employment elsewhere is prevented by legal restraint. Their perpetual insecurity compels Africans to accept any job available, on the terms offered by the employer, or on those laid down by the Minister on the advice of the Wage Board. The nature of this advice is apparent from the Wage Determinations in Table X.

African workers in border factories now suffer the further restraint of insecurity, inflicted on them by Proclamation 74 of March 29, 1968, which limits their employment to yearly contracts, subject to renewal through tribal labour bureaux, administered by government-appointed chiefs and headmen.*

---

*See page 24.

Part Four

The Trade Unions

1. Historical Background

The early history of the South African trade union movement is rich in events of militant endeavour by white workers. In its formative years, there was a vigour and determination which carried workers into nation-wide strikes (in 1913 and 1914) and even rebellion (1922).

The first trade unions were craft unions, started by British immigrants in the latter part of the 19th century. They modelled their unions on the British pattern and some, like the Amalgamated Society of Engineers, even remained part of the British organisation.

In those days there was an endless conflict between the mining companies and its white employees. Because of their great power and wide interests the mineowners were able to influence the general wage structure of the country. Big strikes of white workers took place in mines, railways and industry in 1907, 1911, 1913 and 1914. Soldiers were called out to deal with strikers' demonstrations and in 1914 several strikers were fired upon and killed in the streets of Johannesburg. This strike ended with the arrest of the leaders and the surreptitious deportation of nine of them to England.

The 1922 strike ended in open revolt, with many casualties. The cause of this strike was an attempt by the Chamber of Mines to employ Africans in jobs previously held by whites at lower rates of pay. The whites were defeated; many lost their jobs; most had their wages cut; and the trade unions suffered a temporary setback.

Two years later the white workers got their revenge. The Labour and Nationalist parties joined forces to defeat the ruling South African Party, led by General Smuts (the party of the mineowners), in the 1924 general election. The new Nationalist-Labour pact government immediately restored the colour bar in the mines which had been upset by a court decision* and enacted the Wage Act to protect workers not covered by collective bargaining agreements under the Industrial Conciliation Act.

2. The Wrong Turning

This could have been the opportunity to expand and develop the South African trade union movement by opening its doors to all non-white workers. For various reasons, including race prejudice, fear, suspicion and indifference,

---

*See page 37.

the established unions turned their backs on African workers. Rather than workers' solidarity in non-racial trade unionism, they preferred statutory and conventional colour bars to protect them from cheap African labour competition.

As secondary industry developed, some attempt was made by new industrial unions to embrace African workers and this led to wrangling between them and the craft unions. For many years the issue of non-white membership, bedevilled efforts to establish a central co-ordinating trade union body but in the early 1930s the South African Trades and Labour Council was established. Membership of the Council was open to all races but because little had been done to organise African workers, only a handful of small African unions joined. There were, however, many racially mixed and Coloured unions among the 111 unions which had affiliated by 1947.

In that year, several white, right-wing unions left the Trades and Labour Council following its decision to press for the legal recognition of African trade unions.

In spite of this, it was evident that more trade unionists were recognsing the wisdom and justice of equal trade union rights for all, and were being encouraged by the government's decision to give limited statutory recognition to African trade unions. This promising trend was scotched in 1948 by the success of the Afrikaner Nationalist Party in the general election. From then onwards, the new government steered the unions in the opposite direction, to greater apartheid and firmer exclusion of Africans from trade unionism. As related in Part One, Nationalist policy was to discipline the unions on " Christian-National ", apartheid lines.

The publication of a revised Industrial Conciliation Bill in 1954 revealed the extent to which the government had decided to go to fulfil this policy. A conference of trade unions was hastily summoned to discuss the formation of a new body to fight the new measures. The conference took place in Durban in October 1954, when it was resolved to establish a new federation, to be called the South African Trade Union Council.* By a majority decision the delegates decided to exclude Africans from membership of the Council. To make way for the new federation, the S.A. Trades and Labour Council and the Western Province Federation of Trade Unions were dissolved.

The exclusion of Africans displeased some unions and they decided to establish another co-ordinating body to cater for workers of all races. At a conference held in March 1955 they formed the South African Congress of Trade Unions (Sactu).

These and other federations are dealt with below.

3. Registered Trade Unions

(i) *One in Three Eligible*

The application of the " Christian-National ", apartheid policy over the past 20 years, and the intensification of racially discriminatory practices, have had

*This was later changed to the Trade Union Council of South Africa (Tucsa).

a debilitating effect upon labour organisation. Only 13 per cent of all South Africa's workers are organised in trade-unions.

The scope of recruitment is severely limited because the law does not recognise African workers as employees; unions registered under the Industrial Conciliation Act are barred from having African members. This means that barely one-third of South Africa's economically active population qualify for legal recognition as part of the collective bargaining system.

In mining only 10 per cent of the employees are eligible for membership of the registered trade unions purporting to represent those working in the industry. In manufacturing industry as a whole, scarcely half the employees are eligible; in many industries the proportion is less than 20 per cent.

The limitation on recruitment is not the only obstacle to workers' solidarity and bargaining power. Racialism inside the unions, apathy, rivalry and disunity all help to weaken the movement.

Within the permitted limits, the registered trade unions have fared relatively as well as their counterparts in other countries. But the Trade Union Council (Tucsa) expressed the fear in its 1968 annual report that because of government policies which prevent the organisation of Africans while more of them are being employed, " the trade union concept will disappear from the South African scene ".

According to official statistics the total membership of trade unions registered in terms of the Industrial Conciliation Act at May 1967 was 533,405 in 172 unions. About three-quarters of these trade unionists were classified as white.

Comparative figures of membership, racial composition, and size of the unions are given in Table XI.

Registered trade unions are conceded rights that are denied to Africans but they, too, are circumscribed. Although Coloured* and Asian workers are permitted to belong to registered trade unions, the law denies them equal status with whites. The Industrial Conciliation Act imposes the following restraints:—

- from 1956 onwards the registration of mixed trade unions—i.e. those having both white and Coloured members, or whose membership is open to both white and Coloured persons—is prohibited;
- mixed trade unions, registered before 1956, are allowed to continue but must segregate members in separate racial branches, and hold separate meetings of their white and non-white members. In addition, their executive committees must consist of white persons only and only officials and office bearers may attend or take part in any union meeting of another racial group; failure to observe these requirements results in cancellation of the union's registration;

*For the legal distinctions between the races, see Part Two and footnote page 28.

- no African may be appointed or elected as an official or office bearer, or as a union's representative on an industrial council or conciliation board;

- when members of one race hive off from a mixed union in the whole or any part of the area served by the union and form a new union comprising more than half the members of that race in that area the new union is entitled to claim a share of the assets of the mixed union;

- mixed meetings of shop stewards and mixed congresses or conferences are prohibited;

- mixed trade unions are pegged to their 1965 scope and are not permitted to extend their interests, nor their areas of operation, unless they do so in respect of one race group only.

Besides the above, registered trade unions are also subject to curbs on striking and must accept the job reservation determinations of the Minister of Labour.

It has also been made illegal for trade unions to affiliate to any political party or to sponsor, finance or assist any candidate in a parliamentary or other civic election. Trade unions affiliated to the Labour Party were given six months to resign.

These restrictions made things more difficult for federations such as Tucsa and Sactu, because of their racially mixed membership. These co-ordinating bodies have been handicapped because of other racial laws which put numerous obstacles in the way of conferences, general meetings and other assemblies. It is difficult and sometimes impossible to find hotel accommodation for non-white delegates or places where all delegates can be entertained. The 1967 annual Tucsa conference had to be moved from Port Elizabeth to Cape Town to overcome these restrictions, and officials expressed the fear that " new government moves may put the Council in a position where it could no longer hold multi-racial congresses ".

The effect of the law on the trade union movement has been to divide and weaken it. However, it is noteworthy that in spite of the government's inducements and pressures, the majority of mixed trade unions continue to exist. As can be seen from Table XI there are still 45 mixed unions, representing more than one-third of the total membership of all unions.

(ii) *Rival Federations.*

The disagreements among the registered trade unions over the provisions of the 1956 Industrial Conciliation Act led to the establishment of two more federations, both to the right of Tucsa, viz. the Co-ordinating Council of South African Trade Unions and the South African Federation of Trade

TABLE XI—Trade Unions Registered in terms of the Industrial Conciliation Act

(i) *Number of Unions and membership according to Race.*

Date	No. of trade Unions	Total Membership	Whites	Coloureds	Asians
December 1950	168	355,362	284,076	52,100	19,186
December 1965	168	512,618	367,714	109,290	35,614
May 1967	172	533,405	384,528	148,877	

(ii) *Racial type and membership of Unions.*

	No. of Unions	No. of Members
Membership confined to whites	89	278,931
Membership confined to Coloureds	37	39,225
Mixed white and Coloured membership	46	165,925
	172	484,081

(On June 11, 1968 the Minister of Labour gave the membership of registered trade unions as 533,405, made up of 384,528 whites and 148,877 Coloureds and Asians.)

(iii) *Racial Composition of Mixed Unions.*

Year	No. of Unions	Total Membership	Whites	Coloureds	Asians
1963	47	161,055	85,725	52,660	22,670
1965	45	183,464	92,842	65,141	25,481
1967	46	165,925	81,245	84,680	

(iv) *Size of Unions (1965).*

	Total	White Unions	Coloured Unions	Mixed Unions
Less than 250 members	56	36	13	7
251—500 members	24	8	6	10
501—1,000 members	21	11	4	6
1,001—5,000 members	39	16	11	12
5,001—11,000 members	10	5	3	2
More than 11,000 members	18	10	Nil	8
	168	86	37	45

Source: *Report* 01-56-01 *Labour Statistics: Labour Relations and Trade Unions* 1965–1966; *Bureau of Statistics Pretoria.*

House of Assembly Debates May 16, 1967 *and June* 11, 1968.

Unions. Both these groups supported the government's policies of job reservation, racial separation in the unions and the non-recognition of African unions.

Besides these main groups there was the Federal Consultative Council of South African Railways and Harbours Staff Associations, a combination of the seven associations catering for white workers employed on the government railways and harbours. This body, although claiming to be middle-of-the-road, also accepted the government's policy.*

Finally, there was the South African Congress of Trade Unions (Sactu) which strongly opposed racialism and demanded equal rights for all workers. This federation is dealt with separately, below.

Apart from all the above there were a few unattached unions.

In spite of their fundamental differences, the first four groups agreed in September 1957 to team up in a super-federation called the South African Confederation of Labour. At establishment of the Confederation, the strength of the participants was as follows:—

	Unions	*Affiliated Members*
Trade Union Council of S.A.	34	144,000
S.A. Federation of Trade Unions	12	60,000
Co-ordinating Council of S.A. Trade Unions	13	16,000
Federal Consultative Council of S.A. Railways and Harbours Staff Associations	7	77,000
	66	297,000

The four groups hoped that their alliance would eliminate rivalry in dealings with the government on such issues as the appointment of trade union representatives to public bodies and the selection of workers' delegates to the International Labour Organisation. Tucsa soon discovered that it could not escape the consequences of an alliance with three pro-government, pro-apartheid federations. Inevitably it was under pressure to approve further government measures to tighten restrictions on the unions and extend job reservation. After a year of dissension inside the Confederation on questions concerning the independence and freedom of the separate federations, Tucsa decided at a special conference in Durban on September 15/16, 1958 to sever its connection with the Confederation.

The Confederation continued without Tucsa and by the end of 1967 the line-up was as follows:—

	Unions	*Affiliated Members*
Tucsa	68	166,881 (plus 13 African unions with 6,501 members)
Confederation	33	119,071
Non-Affiliated Unions	71	Unknown

*Railway workers, being State employees, are excluded from the main provisions of the Industrial Conciliation Act; and are subject to the S.A. Railways and Harbours Act. To this extent their staff associations differ from the registered trade unions.

The situation changed again in 1968, however, when internal dissension over African trade union rights resulted in a serious split among Tucsa's affiliates.

The government-orientated Confederation was quick to seize the opportunity and moved in to capture the unions falling away from Tucsa. In June 1968, the Confederation amended its constitution to enable individual unions, as well as federations, to affiliate. At that stage, it claimed to represent nearly 190,000 workers—all whites.

Much of its new strength came from the Co-ordinating Council, whose affiliates were having some organising success, particularly in the engineering and motor industries. One of these affiliates, the S.A. Iron, Steel and Allied Industries Union, has made deep inroads in the field of operation of the Amalgamated Engineering Union and the Boilermakers' Society. Its main platform is opposition to mixed trade unions and denunciation of Tucsa's support for the recognition of African unions. This has found wide appeal among white workers and helped to frighten several Tucsa unions.

The Co-ordinating Council's attitude to non-white workers can be summed up by three recent instances. At its annual congress in August 1968, the Council unanimously resolved that industrial councils should represent whites only, i.e. that even the Coloureds and Indians should be excluded from collective bargaining.[1] In the second instance, a deputation from the Council met Prime Minister Vorster to ask that Republic Day (May 31) be declared a paid holiday every year for *white* workers.[2] In the third, Mr. G. H. Beetge, senior deputy chairman of the Council, stormed out of a cocktail party during the national congress of the Industrial Council for the Building Industry because Coloured and Indian trade union delegates were present.

Mr. Beetge said he would not, as a white man drink with " coolies ", and reported the mixed party to the police.[3]

(iii) *The Rise and Decline of Tucsa.*

As related above the Trade Union Council of South Africa (Tucsa) was born in 1954 as a combination of unions to oppose the government's move, through changes to the Industrial Conciliation Act, to interfere with trade union freedom.

In the effort to bring together the maximum possible number of legally-recognised unions, the leaders chose the expedient course of limiting affiliation to unions registrable under the Act; in other words, excluding African workers.

As most of those present at the foundation of Tucsa well knew, they were merely postponing the day when the real issues of labour organisation would have to be squarely faced. Individual members of Tucsa's executive made various attempts to force the issue of African membership but the body as a whole preferred to avoid it. The reason for this was that the vast majority of members of most unions were in favour of race discrimination and job reservation. The attitude of white wokers on these two issues made it obvious that those trade union leaders who advocated a liberal approach were out of step with the members.

Some progress was made in 1959 when two representatives of the International Confederation of Free Trade Unions (ICFTU) visited South Africa and urged Tucsa to take positive steps to organise African workers. The Tucsa conference of that year resolved " to take the initiative in setting up immediately an independent special committee representative of all racial groups in South Africa for the purpose of organising all workers into trade unions, whether registrable or not ". This was a commitment to organise African workers.

In the three years which followed, the special committee operated infrequently and in a desultory fashion, achieving virtually nothing. However, a few small African trade unions which maintained some liaison with Tucsa unions, joined together to form the Federation of Free African Trade Unions (Fofatusa).

By this time Tucsa was being harassed on the one hand by the conservative appeal of the Confederation and on the other by an increasing loss of face in world trade union affairs.

Confederation unions campaigned among members of the Tucsa unions, especially those with mixed membership, to persuade the whites to break away and form " all white " unions, as desired by the government. Tucsa at that stage was able to withstand this attack from the right. It could not, however, ignore the growing hostility in the ILO; if it continued to exclude Africans from membership, the ILO was sure to reject the credentials of its delegates to conference.

Accordingly, in March 1962, the annual conference of Tucsa decided by 83 to 10, with nine abstentions, to permit properly constituted African unions to become affiliated. By 1965, eight African unions with a total membership of 2,012 had joined.

In this period Tucsa embarked upon a vigorous campaign to build a good public image of itself. Much publicity was given to a declaration (widely distributed in pamphlet form) that Tucsa was " irrevocably opposed to all forms of boycotts, sanctions and politically inspired expulsions from international organisations ". The declaration claimed that evolutionary change in South Africa was much more rapid than it had been in Europe and that " Tucsa is doing all in its power, within constitutional limits, to increase the pace. And it is succeeding ". Tucsa said it needed the understanding and co-operation of fraternal organisations in the Western world, but their support of boycotts and sanctions hampered Tucsa by consolidating the forces of reaction in South Africa.

The 1965 conference, held at East London, struck a highly optimistic note. A four-year blue print, acclaimed by delegates, pointed to an expansion by 1970 to an affiliation of 500,000 workers.

In 1966, the Federation of Free African Trade Unions (Fofatusa) decided to disband and some of its unions linked up with Tucsa, bringing the latter's total African affiliations to 13 with 7,000 members.

An African Affairs section was set up, six African organisers appointed and a course for shop stewards started, and all seemed to be going well, especially as affiliations had grown to 80 unions with more than 200,000 members. But behind the scenes the new liberal policy was causing trouble. The Amalgamated Engineering Union, a foundation member, resigned because it could no longer accept Tucsa's multi-racial policy and other unions were threatening to follow suit. Although a motion at the 1966 conference that Africans be allowed to join registered unions was adopted without a dissenting vote, discussion on the question of African affiliation was conducted behind closed doors and an open break avoided by referring the matter to the incoming executive.

The Minister of Labour saw his opportunity and fanned the fire of disunity by attacking Tucsa publicly with the charge that it was out of touch with South Africa's national viewpoint, particularly in regard to the recognition of African unions and membership of the ILO. This prompted several Tucsa affiliates to demand a change of policy. A special conference was called to review the matter and this took place in December 1967, when it was decided by 51 votes to 13, with 11 abstentions, that Africans be excluded from membership. By this decision, the wheel had turned full circle and after 13 years Tucsa was back where it started. The full resolution read :—

" *In order that the Trade Union Council of South Africa may continue to remain the effective force it has been to date, and in an effort to maintain and increase its present affiliated strength, conference recommends to its affiliates that membership of the Trade Union Council of South Africa be confined to registered trade unions.*

It is the considered opinion of the conference that the Bantu Labour (Settlement of Disputes) Act has failed to stem the tide of Bantu performing semi-skilled and skilled work at greatly reduced rates of pay, whether it be the result of mechanisation, automation or otherwise. This has greatly reduced the bargaining power of the registered trade unions.

The National Executive Committee is instructed by this conference to further pursue with the Minister of Labour the necessity for Bantu workers to be consulted and represented by the registered trade unions and that they be permitted membership of registered trade unions on a basis of limited rights.

Conference requests the Minister of Labour to grant the Trade Union Council of South Africa and other co-ordinating bodies or any registered trade union the right to represent unorganised African workers at Wage Board sittings or to lead evidence on their behalf.

This shall not be construed however, as suggesting a deprivation of the right of African workers to organise and maintain their own unions or present their own evidence at Wage Board proceedings.[4] "

In the anxious days before the decision was taken there were several moves to avoid a showdown. Six of the affiliated African unions were persuaded to resign and four others which were in arrear with their subscriptions were declared to have forfeited their membership. This left Tucsa with three African affiliates when the conference assembled.

The question was debated for two days before a vote was taken. Some of the big unions had forewarned that unless a change was made, they would resign. Awed by this prospect many other unions gave support to the resolution, explaining that they did so for the sake of unity.

As events have shown, Tucsa's decision to revert to its 1954 positon did not " maintain and extend its present affiliated strength ". Barely four months after the December meeting the issue was revived; on April 24, 1968 the fourteenth annual conference reversed the decision of December 1967 and resolved to keep Africans in its ranks. This was agreed by 123,566 votes (56 unions) to 32,871 (18 unions) with 2,518 (3 unions) abstaining.

The Minister of Labour, Mr. Marais Viljoen, reacted at once. The next day he issued a warning that he would use his powers under the Industrial Conciliation Act to cancel the registration of the Trade Union Council if it persisted with the affiliation of African unions.

He followed this up by publicly praising the right-wing, pro-government Mineworkers' Union, saying that he knew it " would go forward to strengthen the arms of fellow rightist workers in other unions in order that the South African trade union movement could become South African in heart and soul ".

He drew a contrast with " certain leftist trade unions who were aiming to organise Africans in trade unions ", accusing them of receiving foreign money to foster this ideal.[5]

Soon afterwards the 15,000-strong Electrical Workers Association withdrew its affiliation. In quick succession, the Amalgamated Society of Woodworkers, two Motor Transport Unions, the Typographical Union, the Amalgamated Union of Building Trade Workers, the Motor Industry Employees Union and others followed suit. By the end of October 1968, Tucsa had lost 10 member unions and faced the prospect of further resignations.

The Minister of Labour congratulated the breakaway unions for showing their support " for the traditional South African pattern of life ". He called Tucsa " un-South African " because it had persisted " in wanting to organise Africans in trade unions in spite of my appeal to them not to do so ". Mr. Viljoen said there were people in Tucsa who had hoped he would introduce legislation to prohibit them from organising African workers, and he would have done so had it been necessary. However, he had first given the white unions a chance to show where they stood and he was happy to see how they had reacted.[6]

These events revealed the tragic plight of Tucsa; although many of those at the top supported a liberal policy, few of them could rely upon the backing of their rank and file on the colour question. The truth of the matter was that all but a few white workers agreed with the government's race policy and the leaders had finally been called to choose between staying with Tucsa or being repudiated by their members.

As 1968 drew to a close, Tucsa was struggling to avoid further defections and even the possibility of a total break-up.

In a desperate effort to keep Tucsa alive, its national executive committee recommended to the 15th annual conference in Johannesburg on February 17-19, 1969 that, once again, Africans should be ineligible for membership. The leadership assured delegates that this third reversal of policy would entice some of the race-sensitive breakaway unions back into the fold. The delegates took the executive's advice and in hopeful anticipation, voted to close Tucsa's doors to African workers.

(iv) *The Rise and Decline of Sactu.*

As related above, the South African Congress of Trade Unions (Sactu) was established in March 1955 by some of the 14 unions which opposed the decision of the 1954 trade union conference that a new federation be formed without Africans. These unions declared that they would continue to struggle " against the policy of racial discrimination and to work for the achievement of a single trade union organisation embracing all sections of the working class ".

At its first annual conference in 1956, Sactu made its political involvement plain ; in contrast to the usual trade union boasts of having nothing to do with politics, Sactu declared :—

> *" Sactu is conscious of the fact that the organising of the mass of the workers for higher wages, better conditions of life and labour is inextricably bound up with a determined struggle for political rights and liberation from all oppressive laws and practices. It follows that a mere struggle for the economic rights of the workers without participation in the general struggle for political emancipation would condemn the trade union movement to uselessness and to a betrayal of the interests of the workers" .*

In pursuance of this declaration, Sactu became a consultative member of the Congress Alliance comprising the African National Congress (ANC), the South African Indian Congress (SAIC), the South African Coloured Peoples' Organisation (SACPO) and the Congress of Democrats (COD). It also signed the Freedom Charter* adopted by these organisations at a mass Congress of the People, held at Kliptown, outside Johannesburg on June 26/27, 1955.

By 1961, Sactu had 46 affiliated unions, representing 53,323 members, of whom 38,791 were Africans. Many of the unions were small but in industries and occupations which previously had not been organised. Besides the normal difficulties in recruiting workers unacquainted with trade unionism, there were the more formidable obstacles arising from the insecurity of African workers and the many laws and regulations which put them at the mercy of their employers and exposed them to punitive action by the authorities at the least sign of involvement with Sactu.

Among other things, Sactu embarked upon a nation-wide campaign for a

---

*The Freedom Charter, based mainly on the United Nations Declaration of Human Rights, set out the demands of the non-white majority for equal rights under ten headings, covering government education, employment, housing, etc. It also demanded a sharing of the country's wealth, through the transfer " to the people as a whole " of the mineral wealth, banks and monopoly industry.

minimum wage of £1 a day. This was widely supported and became the feature of workers' demonstrations.

From 1961 onwards the Congress Alliance was relentlessly persecuted by the authorities and inevitably Sactu suffered. Meetings and conferences of Sactu unions were invaded by the police; union offices were raided; employers were advised to discharge Africans known to be active in the unions; office bearers, officials and organisers were banned from attending gatherings of any kind; and others were jailed without trial under the 90-day law.

Between February and July 1963, no less than 27 Sactu officials (20 Africans, 3 Coloured, 3 whites and one Indian) were prevented from carrying on with their trade union work as a result of bannings and detentions. No sooner had replacements been found than they, too, were banned or detained. Most of the 150 trade union officials removed by government action by the end of 1966 were members of Sactu.

The organisation suffered further because of the arrest and conviction of many rank and file members on charges of belonging to or furthering the aims of the banned ANC, or of offences under the Sabotage Act. Although its forces were severely depleted, Sactu continued to struggle on but eventually was all but wiped out of existence.

4. African Trade Unions.

(i) *Background.*

Only two per cent of African workers in South Africa are organised in trade unions.[7] This is a remarkable state of affairs, considering first that the South African trade union movement is more than 70 years old and second, that African workers were showing a readiness to join unions as long as 50 years ago.

This low level of unionisation is due mainly to (a) racial discrimination in the law and in labour practices; (b) government obstruction and intimidation; and (c) colour prejudice among white workers.

When the first statutory machinery for collective bargaining, the Industrial Conciliation Act, was introduced in 1924, the definition of " employee " was wide enough to allow a large number of Africans to belong to registered trade unions. In 1937, the Act was amended and the definition narrowed to disqualify most of the previously eligible Africans. Some unions allowed their African members to remain but in 1945 the Department of Labour threatened to cancel their registration unless they excluded the Africans.

There followed discussions between the unions and the Smuts government, as a result of which an Industrial Conciliation (Natives) Bill was published in 1947, to provide for separate African trade unions with separate bargaining machinery. Unlike other unions, registration was to be compulsory in the case of African unions and the right to strike severely limited. The Bill was fiercely opposed both by employers and the established unions.

It came to nothing, however, because in 1948, the Nationalist Party came to power, with an entirely different approach to African workers. The new government firmly pegged the Africans to subservience in the Bantu Labour (Settlement of Disputes) Act of 1953, and erected other barriers to end the trend towards wider freedom of organisation. At that stage, there were admitted to be 38,251 paid-up African members of trade unions.[8] (The unions claimed a much larger membership.)

The 1953 law to by-pass unionised Africans and to outlaw strikes by Africans, did not " bleed them to death ", as prophesied by the then Minister of Labour. With the birth of Sactu in 1955 the movement received a new impetus and grew in strength.

In addition to the Sactu unions, there were six satellite African unions attached to the registered unions in the Tucsa group. These unions had a combined membership of about 9,200 in 1958. In the latter half of 1959, as a result of the visit by the two ICFTU representatives, the six satellite unions detached themselves from Tucsa to form the Federation of Free African Trade Unions of South Africa. (Fofatusa).

Although claiming to be non-political, Fofatusa had strong ties with the Pan Africanist Congress (PAC), its chairman, Mr. J. G. Nyaose being a PAC leader (he was later jailed for his PAC activities). Fofatusa was directly affiliated to the ICFTU from whom it received financial assistance.

In 1961, Fofatusa claimed 17 affiliates, representing 18,385 members, but in 1964 the Secretariat gave the the total membership as 14,000. At that stage its main member unions were also affiliated to Tucsa. Fofatusa was at no stage in its existence particularly active and little was heard of it until January 29, 1966, when a general meeting resolved that Fofatusa be dissolved. Announcing this decision, Fofatusa said it was unable to carry on without imperilling its officials, and advised its members to apply for affiliation to Tucsa.

As related above, Tucsa blew hot and cold on African unions until the final showdown with the government in 1968. On establishment in 1954 Tucsa excluded Africans; in 1959 it warmed to the idea of organising Africans; in 1962 it decided to accept African union affiliates; in 1966 it embarked upon a campaign to organise Africans; in 1967 it took an about-turn and once again decided to exclude them; and finally, in April 1968, it took another about turn by reversing the 1967 decision.

After a Tucsa delegation had met him on November 13, 1967, the Minister of Labour, Mr. Viljoen, effectively dashed whatever hopes there were that African unions would get legal status.

He declared:—

" Concerning Tucsa's increasing activities to organise Bantu in trade unions and its sustained insistence that Bantu trade unions must be officially recognised, the attention of the deputation was drawn to the fact that the white workers generally are opposed to such recognition, that the Coloured workers also have reservations about the wisdom of Tucsa's actions and that employers prefer the interests of Bantu workers to be handled as prescribed in the Bantu Labour (Settlement of Disputes) Act.

The Bantu worker himself does not show any great interest in trade unions either. The Bantu Labour Act does not only ensure labour peace but it has also been used, and is still being used with great success, to improve the service conditions of Bantu workers.

In view of the exceptional results which have been achieved with the Act, no justification exists for Tucsa's actions, which constitute a serious danger—as was shown by the manner in which Bantu trade unions were abused by political agitators ".[9]

(ii) *Repression.*

The South African government has not gone to the extent of declaring African trade unions illegal; it has been able to thwart unionisation by other means. But, as the Minister boasted in his clash with Tucsa, had he thought it necessary, he would have brought in a law to prohibit the organisation of African workers.

The government has a vast armoury of laws, regulations and arbitrary power to remove leaders, persecute members and kill African unions. Banning, detention without trial, " endorsing out ", pressure on employers and other weapons are used to subdue those who strive to widen the trade union movement to embrace all South Africa's workers, regardless of race.

Union offices are kept under surveillance and frequently raided by the Special Branch; officials are searched, organisers shadowed and their contacts interrogated; employers are warned to have no dealings with African unions and are informed of " dangerous elements " who should be dismissed; landlords are advised to evict trade union tenants.

Since 1950, African unions have existed under the shadow of the Suppression of Communism Act,* which empowers the government to declare any organisation, including an African trade union (but not other unions) to be an " unlawful organisation " on the grounds that it engages in activites which are calculated to further any of the objects of " communism " as defined in the Act, or that it is controlled, directly or indirectly by any organisation propagating the principles or objects of " communism ".

Among other things, the definition of " communism " includes activities aimed at bringing about an " industrial, social or economic change ". Thus, a strike or any other act organised by a trade union for the purpose of ending job reservation, or gaining higher wages and improved working conditions, could well be declared to be furthering the objects of " communism ", and an excuse to outlaw the union.

Another hazard for African unions is the General Law Amendment Act of 1962, the Sabotage Act. It has a wide definition of " sabotage " under which a strike by Africans could be construed to be a " wrongful or wilful act " to achieve a variety of ends, punishable by the death penalty, or at least a sentence of five years' imprisonment.†

---

*See pages 32 – 33.

†See page 34.

Various laws which control meetings and gatherings, prohibit almost entirely the holding of workers' meetings in the vicinity of their places of work and union organisers are constantly exposed to arrest on charges of trespass. Entry into African townships is controlled by permit and meetings there are subject to permission by white officials.[10] Outside the townships, halls and other public meeting places in urban areas are licensed for the use of whites only. In African areas, meetings of more than ten Africans require official approval in writing, in terms of the Bantu Administration Act. To hold, preside at or address a meeting without the permission of the Secretary for Bantu Administration and Development or his deputy is an offence punishable by a fine up to R200 or 200 days imprisonment.[11]

The Minister of Justice has power under Section 9(3) of the Suppression of Communism Act to prohibit any gathering if he deems this necessary in preventing the achievement of any of the objects of " communism ". As explained above, the wide definition of " communism " could well embrace an African trade union meeting, should the government find the need to resort to such action to suppress a union. The Minister also has power under the Riotous Assemblies Act to prohibit meetings.

In applying repressive measures against union leaders the authorities are able to intimidate African workers, whose position is far more vulnerable than that of other workers. If they lose their jobs because of their trade union activities, Africans are likely to suffer the full fury of South Africa's disciplinary labour laws, described in Part Two. The little security an urban African worker may possess could be snatched away because of his trade union militancy.

The South African Congress of Trade Unions (Sactu) and its affiliated unions endured every form of this persecution until they were finally broken. While these unions were being hammered by the government, it was said that they had invited trouble by taking a political line but it has now been proved by Tucsa's recent experience that " political " means anything contrary to apartheid. As in all other things, the South African government will allow empty talk but it will not tolerate active opposition. As long as Tucsa did no more than pay lip service to the ideal of African unionisation, the government remained passive. But as soon as Tucsa showed signs of doing something, the ire of the government was roused and the Minister stepped in.

(iii) *Unions in Border Areas and Bantustans.*

The right of African workers in border and Bantustan industries to organise and form trade unions has been briefly discussed in Parliament, disclosing the government's complex policy on the subject. The Minister of Labour stated that the establishment and recognition of trade unions in the Bantustans was " their affair ". He said:—

> *" If the Bantu workers in the Transkei want to establish a trade union and if the Transkeian Government recognises the trade union and they have the right to strike, then it is of course their affair. We do not want to prescribe to them how they must regulate their trade unions. Why are*

we then recognising this Bantu area as a state which is capable of making its own laws?"

When the Minister was asked how this affected Africans working in the border factories and living in the Bantustans, he said they would fall under the laws applying to all Africans in white areas and explained:—

> *"The border industries fall under the Republic of South Africa. The Cyril Lord factory in East London for example does not fall under the Transkei. The Bantu workers there are working in the Republic in a White area, and if they work in a White area then they must behave themselves in the same way as the Italians who are working in Swiss factories and who have to obey Swiss laws, are doing . . . a trade union is not a kind of civic society; they cannot live in the Transkei and establish a trade union there if they are working in a White area. Surely a trade union is centred around the site of the factory where one is working?"*[12]

As there are virtually no industries, no significant commercial enterprises in the Bantustans, the Minister's apparent concession is meaningless. It is of no help to Africans to be told they can have trade union rights in distant places where there are no jobs, while such rights are denied to them in the very areas where they are most needed, in the border factories and in the urban industrial areas.

5. The Government Answered.

In his clash with Tucsa, the Minister of Labour advanced four reasons to justify the government's refusal to approve African trade unions:—

1. White workers are opposed to such recognition;
2. Coloured workers have reservations about the wisdom of organising Africans;
3. employers prefer the machinery of the Bantu Labour (Settlement of Disputes) Act;
4. Africans show no great interest in trade unions.

The Minister gave no evidence to substantiate these claims because no facts have been gathered. It is possibly true that a majority of privileged whites are happy with all existing forms of race discrimination, especially those which keep African workers in subservience. It is also possible that a few Coloured people have been infected with the poison of apartheid and would support any measures which keep Africans in an inferior position to themselves, such as allowing them, but not Africans, to belong to trade unions. It may well be that some employers have told the Minister that they are delighted at having the majority of their workers, the Africans, prevented from using the democratic machinery of trade unionism to secure a fairer deal. It certainly is not true to say that Africans are not interested in trade unions.

However, these are not the real reasons for the government's behaviour. The truth is to be found in racial prejudice—a colour prejudice against non-whites, accentuated by a mediaeval white master—black servant attitude.

This is the basis of Nationalist Party policy. It was this appeal to the white electorate which put the Nationalists in power and keeps them there.

The Nationalist oligarchy have made it hazardous to dissent and few are prepared to do anything to displease those in power. For employers, there are the persuasion of government contracts, import permits and other tribute; for white and Coloured workers, the coddling of job reservation and statutory advantages over African workers.

But what of the Africans, the people who are affected by the policy? What have they to say in the matter? The Minister has not even tried to ascertain the views of African workers. The writer, in the course of many years practical experience in South African labour and trade union affairs, found a widespread eagerness among African factory workers to belong to trade unions. Where there was reluctance to join, its causes could be found in employer intimidation and fear of the authorities. Of course, there was a great need for education towards trade unionism before mass unionisation could be expected, but this work was always retarded by obstruction and interference from official sources.

As far back as 1925, the Economic and Wage Commission were informed by Mr. Ivan Walker, who later became Secretary for Labour, that " at no distant date " employers would have to deal with organised African workers.[13] An addendum to the Report of The Native Economic Commission 1930-32, by Mr. F. A. Lucas, declared that there was no good reason for depriving Africans of the benefits of the Industrial Conciliation Act.[14] The Inter-departmental Committee on the Social Health and Economic Conditions of Urban Natives, 1942–43, recommended the registration and administrative recognition of African trade unions.[15] The Witwatersrand Mine Natives' Wages Commission, 1943, agreed that such recognition be given, saying, " The fact of the existence of so many trade unions working for the advancement of Native workers in the large towns is evidence that amongst the more educated and socially advanced classes of Natives there is recognition of the value of trade unionism. That movement is likely to grow and extend. "[16] The Industrial Legislation Commission, 1948–50, also supported the view that African trade unions be legally recognised, but under a separate law from that appertaining to whites and Coloureds.[17] This Commission found that at that stage there were at least 52 African trade unions in existence.

It noted the fact that from 1939 onwards there was a rapid expansion of the African trade union movement but after 1945 there was a decline, because " the desire of Natives to join trade unions had exceeded their ability to control these unions and make use of them ". Among the reasons given for this were the paucity of trained union leaders, the inexperience of the leaders and rank and file, the lack of government recognition and difficulties and setbacks such as those experienced by the movement in Britain in its early stages.

Instead of making an attempt to remedy the deficiencies and encouraging the development of healthy non-racial trade unionism, the government preferred to smash the African trade union movement. Any lack of interest which the Minister finds among Africans today is due to fear of the consequences of forming or belonging to trade unions. The Minister would be nearer the truth if he boasted that his government has successfully blocked the advancement of trade unionism among Africans, in spite of their desires, by vicious, determined acts of repression.

Part Five

South Africa and the World

1. The International Labour Organisation.

South Africa was a member of the International Labour Organisation (ILO) from 1919, the year of its foundation, until March 11, 1966. The last 20 years' membership were increasingly devoted to warding off attacks on apartheid and racial discrimination in the field of labour. In all the time South Africa belonged to the ILO, it ratified only 12 of the 124 Conventions adopted.

Until the end of the Second World War, participation in the ILO had presented no difficulties. Attendance at the conferences in Geneva had been an annual diversion, almost a jaunt, for government, employer and trade union delegates.

With the adoption of the Declaration of Philadelphia in 1944, things changed; the constitution of the ILO acquired a new emphasis. In addition to freedom of expression and association, the right of collective bargaining, the right to work and other rights, was added the principle:—

> " *All human beings, irrespective of race, creed or sex, have the right to pursue both their material well-being and their spiritual development in conditions of freedom and dignity, of economic security and equal opportunity* ".

This struck at the entire labour system in South Africa, which constituted a complete denial of the principle.

In 1947, at the 30th Session of the ILO, Australia, France and India attacked South Africa and demanded a total prohibition on colour discrimination in industrial legislation in all member countries. In 1948, when the ILO considered a draft convention on freedom of association, the South African delegation tried to get support for an amendment which would have sanctioned discrimination against Africans in any guarantee of freedom of association and labour organisation. When their attempt failed the South Africans refused to vote for the draft convention.

In 1954, the International Confederation of Free Trade Unions (ICFTU) protested to the ILO against the Suppression of Communism Act and the Bantu Labour (Settlement of Disputes) Act. In 1955 the ILO Committee on Forced Labour declared South Africa to be one of twelve countries where definite systems of forced labour existed. At the 1955 and 1956 annual conferences, the South African workers' delegate openly attacked the apartheid provisions of the Industrial Conciliation Act, then before parliament. In 1960, the workers' delegate appealed to the ILO to appoint a commission of inquiry into labour conditions in South Africa.

At the 1961 conference, it was resolved, by 163 votes to nil, with 89 abstentions, to call upon South Africa to withdraw from the ILO. When asked to report on the position of law and practice in South Africa in regard to Convention III, Discrimination (Employment and Occupation), the government replied with an involved defence of apartheid.

The Governing Body of the ILO then, at a meeting on June 27-29, 1963, adopted three resolutions on South Africa. The first excluded South Africa from all ILO committees; the second provided for consultations between the Director-General of the ILO and the Secretary-General of the United Nations to seek a solution to the problems arising from South Africa's continued membership; and the third, that consideration be given to amending the ILO Constitution to give effect to the 1961 conference decision.

From this followed a recommendation by the Governing Body that South Africa be presented with an ultimatum to live up to her obligations under the ILO constitution or be suspended. The South African government anticipated the 1964 conference decision on this recommendation by announcing its withdrawal from the ILO. The Minister of Labour stated in parliament on March 11, 1964, that South Africa was leaving because of " an accumulation of hostile acts ".*

Notwithstanding this step, the 1964 ILO conference decided by 253 votes to 24 with 35 abstentions, to adopt the constitutional changes which would allow for the suspension or expulsion of South Africa if it persisted in ignoring the principles of the world body.

2. ILO Declaration and Programme on Apartheid.

On July 8, 1964 the International Labour Conference unanimously adopted a *Declaration concerning the policy of apartheid of the Republic of South Africa.* On the same day the conference unanimously approved recommendations made by the Governing Body in its *ILO Programme for the Elimination of Apartheid in Labour Matters in the Republic of South Africa.*

The Declaration charged South Africa with having persistently and flagrantly violated the principle of equal opportunity for all human beings, irrespective of race, by means of legislative, administrative, and other measures incompatible with the fundamental rights of man, including freedom from forced labour, freedom of association, and freedom of choice of employment and occupation.

It reaffirmed the ILO's " condemnation of the degrading, criminal and inhuman racial policies of the Government of the Republic of South Africa ", and called upon South Africa :—

---

*The resignation became effective only two years later, in terms of the ILO constitution.

- " to renounce without any further delay its policy of *apartheid* and, in like manner, to repeal all legislative, administrative and other measures which are a violation of the principle of the equality and dignity of man and a direct negation of the inherent rights and freedoms of the peoples of South Africa;

- to establish and consistently to pursue the policy of equal opportunity and treatment for all, in employment and occupation, irrespective of race;

- to repeal, without delay, the statutory provisions which provide for compulsory job reservation or institute discrimination on the basis of race as regards access to vocational training and employment;

- to repeal, without delay, all legislation providing for penal sanctions for contracts of employment, for the hiring of prison labour for work in agriculture or industry, and for any other form of direct or indirect compulsion to labour, including discrimination on grounds of race in respect of travel and residence, which involves racial discrimination or operates in practice as the basis for such discrimination;

- to repeal, without delay, the statutory discrimination on grounds of race in respect of the right to organise and to bargain collectively, and the statutory prohibitions and restrictions upon mixed trade unions including persons of more than one race, and so to amend the Industrial Conciliation Act that all workers, without discrimination of race, enjoy the right to organise and may participate in collective bargaining ".

In terms of the Declaration, the Director-General of the ILO was asked to submit a special report every year on developments in labour matters in South Africa and the application of the Declaration, including recommendations concerning the measures which should be taken with a view to ending apartheid.

The *ILO Programme for the Elimination of Apartheid in Labour Matters in the Republic of South Africa,* covered three aspects of labour policy:—

- equality of opportunity in respect of admission to employment and training;

- freedom from forced labour (including practices which involve or may involve an element of coercion of labour);

- freedom of association and the right to organise.

Under each of these headings the Programme dealt with (a) the general situation in South Africa; (b) particulars of relative legislation; (c) the findings of the Committee of Experts and the Conference Committee on the application of ILO Conventions and Recommendations; and (d) recommendations for action.

South Africa was told exactly what steps should be taken and which specific laws should be repealed or amended to eliminate the racial discrimination affecting the employment opportunities, earnings and trade union rights of South African workers. The final paragraph reads:—

> "150. Changes so far-reaching would inevitably involve a complete recasting of labour legislation, social services and industrial relations in the Republic of South Africa. In the formulation of further plans for this purpose, designed to achieve the objective indicated by the resolution unanimously adopted by the Security Council of resolving the present situation in South Africa, with the co-operation of the Government of South Africa, 'through full, peaceful and orderly application of human rights and fundamental freedom to all inhabitants of the territory as a whole, regardless of race, colour or creed, the International Labour Organisation should be prepared to play an appropriate part in co-operation with the United Nations.'"

3. From ILO to UN.

Following upon South Africa's withdrawal from the ILO, the issues were referred to the United Nations, in terms of procedure laid down by the UN Economic and Social Council for dealing with allegations against member states of the UN which were not members of the ILO.[1]

The first matter to be referred by the ILO to the United Nations was a complaint from the World Federation of Trade Unions in July 1966. The Secretary-General of the UN advised the South African government of the complaint and received a reply that the matter was solely within the jurisdiction of South Africa. The matter was then handed over to the UN Economic and Social Council, which instructed the Commission on Human Rights to request its Working Group of Experts to investigate the infringement of trade union rights in South Africa.[2]

The Working Group held two sessions, one in Geneva and the other in New York and submitted its report on February 2, 1968.[3]

It concluded that:—

> "The international standards relating to trade union freedoms are being seriously and persistently violated by South African legislation and by administration and penal measures. These violations result in racial discrimination between African workers and trade unionists on the one hand, and non-African workers and trade unionists on the other. They are a manifestation of the policy of apartheid, which, in its efforts to separate the races, undeniably discriminates between the different groups of workers and trade unionists".

In addition to recommending changes in law and practice the Working Group declared that the South African Government "must refrain from prosecuting African workers and trade unionists because of their trade union activities on the pretext that they have committed violations of ordinary law . . ."

The Secretary-General of the United Nations, U Thant, stated in his address to the assembly of heads of State and government of the Organisation of African Unity (OAU) in Algiers on September 13, 1968:—

> " The continuing enforcement by the South African Government of its policies of *apartheid,* including recent attempts to extend the philosophy of racial discrimination and segregation to neighbouring territories, has given rise to a loss of faith in many quarters in the possibility of peaceful evolution towards a society based on justice and equality. At the same time, while the United Nations has been engaged in wide ranging efforts to deal with this situation, in co-operation with the specialised agencies and with non-governmental organisations, Member States have felt increasingly disappointed at the relative ineffectiveness of the United Nations so far. Indeed, recent developments point to the danger of violence which, though limited in scope at this stage, might well have grave consequences for the future of that part of the world and for international harmony. The chances of averting this danger depend essentially on the willingness of the great Powers and the major trading partners of South Africa to persuade the South African Government to abandon its present course ".

This points to the real reason why South Africa is able to maintain its defiance of both the ILO and the UN. Although the nations of the world collectively denounce apartheid and produce an endless flow of resolutions demanding action, separately many of them maintain cordial relations and flourishing trade with South Africa.

Through direct investment and subsidiary establishments, the principal industrialists of leading UN member states are in fact, sharing in the profits of apartheid exploitation.

LIST OF TABLES

REFERENCES

PART ONE.

1. House of Assembly Debates, March 19, 1942.
2. Ibid. January 19, 1943.
3. *Die Kruithoring* (official Nationalist Party newspaper) June 1943.
4. *Die Transvaler* July 4, 1944.
5. Act No. 44 of 1950.
6. House of Assembly Debates, March 19, 1968.
7. Ibid. June 7, 1968.

PART TWO.

1. Senate Debates, June 7, 1954.
2. House of Assembly Debates, June 17, 1959.
3. Report of the Local Government Commission, U.G. 62/1921.
4. Union Statistics 1910–1960, Bureau of Census and Statistics, Pretoria.
5. Report of the Commissioner of the South African Police, R.P. 39/1967.
6. *The Star* Johannesburg, August 10, 1968.
7. *Evening Post* Port Elizabeth, October 19, 1968.
8. *Rand Daily Mail* Johannesburg, January 19, 1968.
9. House of Assembly Debates, June 18, 1968.
10. Senate Debates, June 20, 1955.
11. House of Assembly Debates, February 6, 1968.
12. Proclamation R. 74, March 29, 1968—*Government Gazette Extraordinary* No. 2029.
13. Report of the Commissioner of the South African Police, R. P. 39/1967.

PART THREE.

1. House of Assembly Debates, May 8, 1964.
2. Iron, Steel and Metallurgical Industry, Main Agreement; Government Notice No. R. 632, April 19, 1968
3. Suppression of Communism Act, 1950, Section 1 (i) and (ii).
4. Ibid. Section 2(3).
5. *Evening Post* Port Elizabeth, August 13, 1966.
6. General Law Amendment Act (Act No. 76 of 1962).
7. ILO Programme for the Elimination of Apartheid in Labour Matters in the Republic of South Africa, Geneva 1964.
8. House of Assembly Debates, October 11, 1966.
9. Ibid. March 12, 1968; March 22, 1968; April 2, 1968.
10. Act No. 12 of 1911.
11. Act No. 27 of 1951.
12. House of Assembly Debates, May 16, 1967.
13. Ibid. April 5, 1968.
14. *Sunday Times* Johannesburg, April 9, 1967.
15. *Evening Post* Port Elizabeth, October 16, 1968.
16. House of Assembly Debates, June 4, 1968.
17. *Rand Daily Mail* Johannesburg, September 19, 1968; *The Star* Johannesburg, September 21, 1968.
18. *Die Transvaler* Johannesburg, September 23, 1968.
19. Printing and Newspaper Industry, Amendment of Main Agreement, Government Notice R. 1347, August 1968.
20. *Evening Post* Port Elizabeth, September 28, 1968; October 1, 1968; October 2, 1968.
21. Determination No. 14, Durban and Pietermaritzburg; Determination No. 24, East London.
22. *Rand Daily Mail* Johannesburg, October 8, 1968.
23. House of Assembly Debates, March 8, 1968.
24. *Sunday Times* Johannesburg, April 2, 1967.
25. *Rand Daily Mail* Johannesburg, September 26, 1968; *Evening Post* Port Elizabeth, September 28, 1968; October 5, 1968.
26. *Cape Times* Cape Town, October 9, 1968.
27. *Natal Mercury* Durban, September 30, 1968.
28. Nursing Act (Act No. 69 of 1957).
29. House of Assembly Debates, April 4, 1967.
30. *Rand Daily Mail* Johannesburg, May 27, 1968.
31. House of Assembly Debates, March 20, 1968.
32. *Rand Daily Mail* Johannesburg, May 27, 1968.
33. *Dagbreek en Landstem* Johannesburg, November 24, 1968.
34. Government Notice R. 1297, July 26, 1968.
35. *Rand Daily Mail* Johannesburg, October 23, 1968.

36. Convention 111, Discrimination (Employment and Occupation), Forty-first Session, ILO, Geneva 1958.
37. House of Assembly Debates, June 4, 1968.
38. Act No. 53 of 1946.
39. Act No. 41 of 1949.
40. Act No. 9 of 1957.
41. Act No. 30 of 1941.
42. Survey of Race Relations 1967, South African Institute of Race Relations, Johannesburg.
43. Act No. 22 of 1941.
44. *Financial Mail* Johannesburg, May 10, 1968.
45. Ibid. December 13, 1968—Special Survey: Coal.
46. *Rand Daily Mail* Johannesburg, July 21, 1968.
47. *Financial Mail* Johannesburg, February 23, 1968.
48. *Business Times* (*Sunday Times*) Johannesburg, September 1, 1968.
49. *Sunday Times* Johannesburg, September 15, 1968.
50. *Financial Mail* Johannesburg, February 2, 1968.
51. *Evening Post* Port Elizabeth, March 1, 1968; May 1, 1968.
52. House of Assembly Debates, June 4, 1968.

PART FOUR.

1. *Rand Daily Mail* Johannesburg, August 27, 1968.
2. *Evening Post* Port Elizabeth, October 31, 1968.
3. *Die Beeld* Cape Town, August 4, 1968.
4. *Rand Daily Mail* Johannesburg, December 13, 1967.
5. Ibid. May 27, 1968.
6. Ibid. September 10, 1968.
7. *Financial Mail* Johannesburg, August 4, 1967.
8. Report of the Industrial Legislation Commission, U.G. 62/1951.
9. *Rand Daily Mail* Johannesburg, November 14, 1967.
10. Government Notice R. 1036, June 14, 1968.
11. Proclamation R. 268, 1968—*Government Gazette Extraordinary* No. 2165, September 20, 1968.
12. House of Assembly Debates, October 11, 1966.
13. Report of the Economic and Wage Commission, 1925 U.G. 14/26.
14. Report of the Native Economic Commission 1930–32, UG. 22/1932.
15. Report of the Inter-Departmental Committee on the Social, Health and Economic Conditions of Urban Natives, 1942–43.
16. Report of the Witwatersrand Mine Natives' Wages Commission, U. G. 21/1944.
17. Report of the Industrial Legislation Commission, U. G. 62/1951.

PART FIVE.

1. Resolution 277 (X), February 17, 1950.
2. Resolution 1216 (XLII), June 1, 1967.
3. Report of the Ad Hoc Working Group of Experts, E/4459, February 15, 1968.